THE HEREAFTER

Also by Jeanette Dowdell

Something For Everyone With Love (poetry)
Heavenly Mysteries (children's book)

THE HEREAFTER

Our Next Assignment, Our Next Grand Adventure

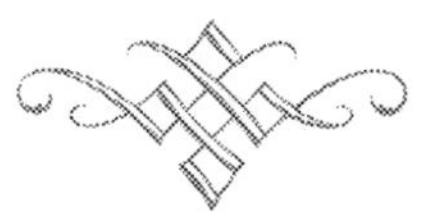

JEANETTE DOWDELL

iUniverse LLC
Bloomington

THE HEREAFTER
Our Next Assignment, Our Next Grand Adventure

iUniverse books may be ordered through booksellers or by contacting:

iUniverse LLC
1663 Liberty Drive
Bloomington, IN 47403
www.iuniverse.com
1-800-Authors (1-800-288-4677)

ISBN: 978-1-4759-9716-3 (sc)
ISBN: 978-1-4759-9721-7 (hc)
ISBN: 978-1-4759-9720-0 (ebk)

Printed in the United States of America

iUniverse rev. date: 08/14/2013

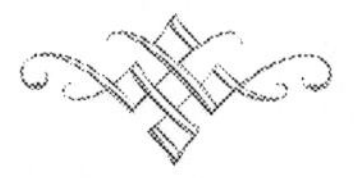

CONTENTS

Dedication vii
Acknowledgements ix
Introduction xi

Searching 1
"What Do I Do Now?" 21
"A Fantastic Journey" 35
"Absurd, More Absurd, Most Absurd, And Beyond Absurd" 87
"Everlasting Life, Shoreless Sequels" 97

Bibliography 113
Author's Biography 117

"Can God's home be any less beautiful than Earth, which He created for us?

Jeanette Dowdell

Dedication

I lovingly dedicate this book to those who knew me best

Mabel G. Barton Dowdell, mother
John R. Dowdell, brother

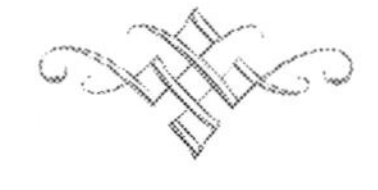

ACKNOWLEDGEMENTS

My Friends

They listen, they hear, and offer endless support,
encouragement, and suggestions

Florence and William Facibene
Ann Glorioso
Marilyn Ike
Judy K. Meserve*
Ruth B. Overton*
Gladys Sollitto
Rosemaria Waegerle

* *Special thanks to Judy and Ruth for their additional dedication, research and multiple reviews*

I would be remiss if I did not express extra special gratefulness to Judy Meserve for the unselfish giving of her time for reading, re-reading, and sharing of her expertise while assisting me during the endless and tedious task of proof-reading and editing. She never tired no matter how many times I corrected and changed the contents within each chapter. Judy was as tenacious as I. For her patience, interest and friendship my heartfelt thanks.

Introduction

Yes! There are hundreds of questions in this book. But, I find that to be nothing less than the start of something good. After all, the topic lends itself to questions, doesn't it?

Let's begin with one of the most profound, "Who would not want to know where they will be going after they die?"

I have discussed this question with various people over the course of many years. Some of their thoughts and visions are included in this book. Many of them overlapped, but not one specifically mirrored my own. That is one of the reasons I decided to pen my thoughts and beliefs. In addition, I personally, have always found the topics of "life after death" and the "Hereafter" not only fascinating and frightening, but somewhat comforting.

This multi-media presentation attempts to seriously define these topics, while adding some humor and tongue-in-cheek thoughts. The book includes a short story, some poetry, conversations with God, and an oft questioned Bible quote, which I believe I have answered.

While travelling through this adventure, you will journey with a character experiencing an unexpected out-of-body trip through deep space. You will feel his excitement as he defines his travels in a state of awe. That journey will include short planetary explanations that are filled with beauty and joy. Hopefully, they will leave you with a powerful desire to stay in that peaceful atmosphere. Perhaps even want to delve deeper into each topic. I hope the Heavens that are filled with endless void and still to be discovered answers renew and intrigue you enough to elevate your interest to its highest heights, as you rediscover one of God's ultimate creations. May His glorious playground of unanswered questions regarding the why, the how, the when, the what, of His magnificent gift to us all become a challenge in your future.

You might even ask yourself as you journey, "Have we been created for a specific purpose, or are we simply a continuation of experimentations whirling in time and place? Do we represent a line of past history, now floating and perhaps drifting free of our ancestral past? Are we a new generation of that life past, or simply the beginning of one in the process of being developed? Are our lives and our existence a farce, an absurd endeavor? One thing is for certain. If you believe it will be everlasting, then it will smack of Bing!

Yes, there are some absurd moments in this book that put forth some unexpected requests, ideas and thoughts that will make you smile and even possibly say about the author, "How could she?" But that is what makes the journey brim with fact, fiction, fantasy, fun and faith.

I'm sure many will ask, "Are you qualified to write this book?" My answer, I am as qualified as anyone else who has ever attempted to write about the Hereafter. What do I base my qualifications upon?—my life, my deep faith, and all the experiences of those who shared their influential and inspiring thoughts—those who have truly touched my heart and spirit—those who spoke to my soul without knowing the power of their own presence. I interviewed many people of many faiths to ascertain their beliefs. I interviewed non-believers also. There were some who I interviewed who immediately stated, "I'm not religious, nor have I ever given life after death a thought." I found that to be strange. Why not simply say, "I don't know, or I don't care."

Actually, my purpose has always been to brighten your day, give you plenty of food for thought and topics for discussion. Truly that is my intent. But as you journey with me remember a simple basic fact. Given the topic, almost everyone is searching for answers, just as I did. I have found my answers. Answers that I can live with, answers that led me to say, "I know where I will be going when I die." However to further clarify my belief, I will continue to search and I invite you to join me. Let's travel together.

Let me ask you "Are you looking for something special with regard to life after death and the Hereafter? I know you'll find it. Just keep searching.

Searching

The Hereafter
Our Next Assignment, Our Next Grand Adventure

> Why should anyone read this book? Sheer curiosity, or to end the searching for answers to your questions regarding life after death

Actually, I have written this book for those who believe in the Hereafter—those who wish to find comfort in the thought of an everlasting tomorrow—those who believe, but have a need of reassurance—those who are wracked with curiosity and have reached the end of their searching tether—those who say, "Why bother to waste the time—to give that thought any thought! After all, no one has ever given me a satisfactory answer about life after death and the Hereafter." O, how often I have heard that and similar comments over the course of my adult life.

But now, I base my belief on fact. The message about life after death and the Hereafter was delivered by God through His Son. Here are some facts to think about. As Jesus hung on the cross with a thief on each side, one said, ***"Jesus, remember me when you come into your kingdom." Jesus answered him, "I tell you the truth, today you will be with me in paradise." Luke 23:42-43 (NIV-New International Version).***

Fact, Jesus lived. Fact, Jesus healed. Fact, Jesus preached. Fact, Jesus even in His dying reiterated The Promise he made earlier about life after death and the Hereafter. He comforted

His Disciples, saying, ***"In my Father's house are many rooms; if it were not so, I would have told you. I am going there to prepare a place for you." John 14:2 (NIV—New International Version).***

For many, this statement then leads to more questions. Some refer to the place in the Father's house as rooms; others define it as a mansion; still others define it as a mansion with many rooms. Throughout this book, I will try to clarify what this means. You will come to know the meaning of these words and how they apply to all of us who believe. The meaning rests in my belief and conclusion.

Let me start with the premise that the Hereafter can be anything you want it to be. Can you live with that answer? The answer to life after death, the Hereafter and any doubt does not take away from where it comes. The belief usually arises out of faith—curiosity—imagination and other's thoughts and teachings. I have written a poem to address these thoughts. It is entitled:

"THAT'S THE TOMORROW YOU'LL SEE"

When you receive tomorrow's call,
Will you shudder and prostrate fall?
Will fear swirl, not knowing where you will be going?
What seeds, if any, you will be sowing?
After all, life as you know it will change forever,
Humanity, your world and you, will no longer be tethered together,
What lies ahead is hidden from view,
What if anything might you be asked to do?
Rest, and rest, and sleep on, in an everlasting state,
Or will you in spirit move on to constantly migrate,
Each one's journey will belong to him; it's his alone,
But, will it really be one self-sown?

Or, will the power that gave you, life and birth,
determine its worth?
Give you another life, in space, or on another *earth*?
Will your afterlife, your "Hereafter,"
meet your expectations?
Will it be a moment of renewal and celebrations?
Or, will it simply be the end of the saga—
your book; the final page?
After all, the story is finished—
you have stepped off that stage,
It is your time to move on—
play new scenes in the vast unknown,
That place of peace, and rest, and fantasies
overblown?
I believe whatever you envision
"The Hereafter" to be . . .
That's the tomorrow you'll see

Life after death is not a new thought. It has been around for centuries. However, it has not been well defined. Think about it. How is it classified? Is it fact, fiction, fantasy, or fun? That depends upon your faith—how deep—how serious—how ingrained. Actually, how you feel about God, your Maker. What you believe Him to be. Unapproachable, or as close as the breath you breathe.

Much of what people believe has been learned in childhood, and then adopted. It has been passed on by others, who by the way, have lived under the same historical learning umbrella. You know the billions who have undergone the same process of indoctrination. But, like the roots of a thirsty tree, some have reached out in search of deeper nourishment. They have as I, been searching for answers to questions that seem to have no answers. Could that uncertainty be because of the world's overall lack of knowledge on the subject? Over the millennia, the subject of life after death has remained one of God's greatest mysteries—a mystery yet to be solved. And for some reason, many people believe in the Hereafter, but have deep doubts about life after death. Thus they continue searching.

Why should the Hereafter exist, if not to serve a purpose? And why shouldn't one of its purposes be to support life after death?

I know the answers that I have received about life after death and the Hereafter have lacked substance and relevance. They can be challenged, and are, but without any new responses and insight. Most of the answers given by professionals, those who are called upon for insight, very often do not increase our faith and boost our confidence. In fact, they don't seem to expand our understanding and knowledge. Most times, they tell us what they believe we want to hear. What we will be most comfortable with in the resolution of our questions. They try to eliminate our fear of tomorrow's unknown. Since they are not seers, fortune tellers, or mediums, their answers are equal to everyone else's suppositions and assumptions. And since I have not, over the course of my lifetime, been satisfied with having received a logical answer about the Hereafter and my place in it, I have drawn my own conclusions. And I find them to be most logical. Why do I continue searching? I want to be better able to share my belief.

But, who am I? How about another cog in humanity's wheel? Suffice it to say, I am happy to share with you and anyone else who will listen, my belief. Some may find it laughable; others may find comfort in my thoughts. As I mentioned before, I base my belief on fact, and the message that was clearly delivered by God through His Son.

My belief is basic and very simple.

I am part of God, and God is part of me, just as God is part of everything. Nothing exists that has not been touched by His hand. That is why, if I fail to do right, or act in an unacceptable manner, I reproach myself and feel I have failed my Maker. I do not need a Dante's world of fear, pain and suffering in order to lead an acceptable life. I know what is expected of me. I know what my responsibilities as given should be, and how they should be intertwined in my life. I know what I want my life after death to be, and with whom I wish to spend it. I am sure it is no less than what everyone else hopes for and wants.

As we all know, there are so many beliefs about life after death that they are too many to innumerate. However, I find the most depressing to be, "When you die, you die. It's over—that is the end." Thank God, there are others like me who have deeper, more beautiful thoughts, such as the continuation of life after death. But, even those who embrace such thoughts never seem to define that life. What kind of life? Where? What are the specifics? Trust me, I will identify that life, and be most specific later in this book.

I gave it years of thought, then I slipped into retrospective mode, and like a snowball running downhill, I gained greater curiosity. And when my curiosity got the best of me, I began to seriously investigate life after death and the Hereafter. I conducted interviews with friends, acquaintances and strangers about these related topics. I asked them, "When you die, what do you think will happen to you?" And, "What do you expect to find in your Hereafter?" Some people were very interested and answered freely and openly. Two of my closest friends, Mabel and Ruth, were most direct and logical. They answered without hesitation and with definite assuredness by saying, "I DON'T KNOW."

Most, including one of my long-time beloved teachers stated such things as: being in a place of beauty, comfort, happiness, a place filled with love, where they will dwell with angels, find their parents, family members and friends. Many felt that they would be reunited with ***everyone*** they ever knew who went on before them. Some mentioned what they would be wearing in their ethereal surroundings—a flowing white gown and large wings, and being perfectly content. A couple of interviewees just needed more time to think about it and draw a conclusion. Another indefatigably believed that she would have to undergo a purification period, be judged by Jesus and spend time in Purgatory.

There were many however, who declined to answer, or even become involved in a discussion on the subject. I wondered whether or not they were afraid. Obviously, I accepted their declination, and respected them for their honesty. After all, everyone's tomorrow is very private and personal. Isn't it? I did appreciate all those who took the time to think about my questions and answer them. But I still cannot help feeling sorry for those who believe living beyond today is unbelievable and impossible. They either have given up searching, or have accepted someone else's thoughts that appealed to them.

Now don't be shocked. I not only believe in life after death in the Hereafter, but life beyond it—Life, ad infinitum—EVERLASTING. And I feel this book best expresses why I feel that way. I know where I came from, and I know where I am going. I feel secure in my belief about my tomorrow. Is there doubt? No. Are there questions? There will always be questions. So, I leave your thoughts to you. What do you really think about your tomorrow? Are you searching? Have you been searching? You are welcome to share my belief. In fact, I would be delighted. I want you to know where you will be and where we will be able to find each other in our life after death in the Hereafter.

I am sure what I believe has merit. It is possible. And, it answers an age-old question which pertains to the well-known and often quoted Biblical passages—***Luke 23:42-43 NIV-New***

International Version and John 14:2 NIV-New International Version, mentioned prior. I hope you will find some comfort in my thoughts, and my belief regarding Jesus' words and "The Promise."

Isn't it amazing, that when we are young and on the upside hill of life, we do not think about death. But the norm is still true, as we age and face the downside hill of life, the inevitable thoughts of passing and death magnify. Our searching for our tomorrow intensifies, as we reach for future solace and peace. As we mentally walk more aware in the very time that is beyond our control.

Today, I personally have millions of thoughts about life after death and the Hereafter, and each is fighting to obtain recognition for a higher level juxtaposition. So, I am writing these thoughts for all to see. Please join me in my *Tomorrowland.* It is a land of promise, a land in which you can believe in the everlasting, or dismiss it. It is all up to you. My searching has been rewarded. I have found my niche—my everlasting life, and I am ready to share my belief and feelings not only with you, but with the world. Hopefully, somewhere along the way, I will bring not only some solace to those who find the subject distressing, but some laughter, or at least a chuckle or two, to all. But in doing so, a question arises. Where should I begin?

Everlasting darkness,
Everlasting light,
Everlasting depression,
Everlasting joy,
Everlasting hope . . .

The choice is yours, whether learned or created, your *Tomorrowland* can be a black hole of nothingness, or a never-ending everlasting light-filled with all the imagination, creativity, sharing and giving as yet known to the human spirit.

It can be an extension of everything good that is housed in the human mind and body. For the black hole of tomorrow is the black hole of yesterday, and soon they both will be the black hole of forever, when they become part of history.

Let me ask you, "How do you find light, when you are walking in light? Do you consider the degrees, the shades, and the depths of the light itself?" But, there is no problem finding a light when you are walking in darkness and a light suddenly appears. Therefore, you can only understand the true beauty of light, my tomorrow, if you come out of darkness, and walk into the light.

Today, are we walking in light, facing darkness? Or, are we walking in darkness, facing the brightest of lights yet known to man? How little we know, and how much we think we know. That to me is amazing. How often have you heard, and read about people who have died and come back from Heaven with one message. They all remember and emphasize a bright light. Brighter than any they had ever experienced in life. Did it illuminate a scene that they will remember in life and be able to recall it from memory later on? Maybe that's why some people, as well as I have said, "I think that I have been here before. It's familiar, but I don't know why." And that fits into my theory of life after death. When I reveal where you and I will be going, it will be very obvious. It underscores life after death and the possibility of another Assignment.

I feel that life after death will be filled with endless possibilities—ones filled with "luminosities" on multi-unknown levels. And they will be well beyond our human conception. Without a doubt, the knowledge we have gained during this lifetime will provide us with new strength to meet the demands of Our Next Assignment, Our Next Grand Adventure. We will have time to review and build on our old experiences. Will our inability to reach beyond the confines of our present mental capacity, our known boundaries and parameters, limit us? That remains to be seen. Also, all of this will depend upon our ability to continue to think and reason. Will it not?

My belief regarding my "Hereafter mind" comes in the form of a question. "In that environment, why should my mind be anything less than its potential?" What do you think?

To gain some insight, ask those around you, what they think and believe about life after death. Then expand it to include "the mind." The answers you receive will surprise you. But always be ready to answer them, when they turn the question back to you.

Continuing on, ask those who deny the Hereafter and life after death, "Is your logic based upon fear? Fear of believing in something that has not as yet ever been proven to exist? Or, have you secretly created something that works better for you—something that no one has ever been able to refute or satisfactorily explain? Perhaps you are disengaged, or disenchanted by the possibility of the very existence of an afterlife? Have you ever found total comfort within your own answers to the afterlife question? Where did they come from? Can you apply the answers to all who have ever been, or who have yet to be born?"

I rarely received any answers to these questions. I was tuned out—turned off. Perhaps they could not apply a positive, logical explanation. However, I do hope that they began to rethink their thoughts.

It was at this point that I began to think about the billions, perhaps trillions of bones, in countless cemeteries that could attest to having lived. Are their spirits/souls still attached to their bones? Could be, but who knows. Or have their spirits as most believe, risen to higher heights? Risen to a place, or places unknown? Risen to a sacrosanct world of forever?

Do the bones of those who did not hold a belief in life after death die with their bodies, no spirit—ending life as they knew it, and the thought of a forever afterlife? And whose belief is right? Those who believe in Everlasting Death? Or, those who believe in Everlasting Life? Again, I must repeat, who knows?

Why should I feel so strongly about my tomorrow? Why do I know where I am going after death and why I am going there? It seems to have a definite purpose. Why am I so "bloody" sure and comfortable with my belief? It's not only a comfort for tomorrow, but also one for today. Perhaps it is because I have searched so long.

I must be perfectly honest. There are two things bothering me. I can't take anything with me. No, I don't mean household items. They won't fit in the hearse. My concern, what if I don't outlive my "pet." Who will take care of that situation in the future?

And too, I would like to retain my ability to whistle. I will be at a loss without that, and it certainly won't take up any room. Why do I need my whistle you might ask? Well, if I whistle, my family, pets, friends, associates, etc. will all know for sure it's me. Maybe I should put in a request now. That's not a bad idea, is it? Enough, I digress. Let me return to the serious.

Where are your deceased loved ones? Are they resting in their dirt beds? Or, are their spirits mingling with all those who have ever lived on earth and/or elsewhere? Can their spirits be divided to accommodate a place in our hearts and Another Assignment, Another Grand Adventure? How about that thought, the thought of Another Assignment—Another Grand Adventure? What do you really think about that? And why do I feel so strongly about that concept? One reason I believe it to be so powerful is that I don't believe God would waste His time on creating intricate creatures such as humans to let them live such short lives. In fact, I find that extremely hard to believe.

Now, when I say that, I am not thinking about reincarnation. No. Not within the realm of its present definition—the birth of a soul in a new body, or a person in whom a soul is believed to have been born again. No. I believe "our spirit" is "our spirit" ad infinitum. Our spirits live an everlasting life. We don't give up our souls. We keep them as we journey into other assignments. They are our spirits. We remain who we are, but not necessarily as we were. Identifiable, yes! We will always be identifiable by our spirits. We are our souls forever.

For now of course, we can only think in human terms, and those terms are as limited as our knowledge and experience. But put our spirits back where they came from, with our Creator, and the possibilities are endless and limitless, as limitless as the universe or universes that now exist. Not just those we know about, but those that may and do exist beyond our imaginations—as limitless as space itself—the very space that is now expanding as we breathe. We are so much less than the smallest grain of sand or an invisible particle yet to be discovered, let alone named, unless we consider something scientists are confident they have recently rediscovered after a half-century quest—a Higgs boson, the elusive subatomic speck sometimes called the "God's particle."

Ordinary people, like me, define things in ordinary ways. An atom is an atom—defined by man as the smallest particle of a chemical element that can exist. Let's not forget the "nano"—atom. It is smaller still. Now, split that into billions or trillions of parts. The question then wanting an answer is, "Where do we fit into creation, into the "The Big Bang" equation with its quarks and gluons?" The answer is beyond calculable, beyond fathomable. Tie that into Jesus' statement that "in my Father's house there are many rooms . . ." Doesn't that open up a new understanding of tomorrow? "The Promise" in that statement is far greater than most have ever imagined, or even have given thought to. The limitlessness of that thought is in itself unbelievable. There are no walls in God's house or mansion—just space and sky and any other terms that we may apply to new findings. Think about where the application is coming from—humanity, one invisible particle of creation. Obviously, that brings me to another point, Creation itself. I do not believe in all the scientific theories about creation, including the Big Bang. That theory is like reaching for the stars. And there are too many of those to be captured. Did you know that we all have some stardust as part of our being? That we do, and apparently scientists have proven it. Love it!

Ah, yes, the Big Bang Theory. The origin of the Universe . . . Hello! It created something, or everything out of nothing. We all began. Really! Okay, it might have started something. But what, or who created the minutest details of each living thing—each inanimate object—does it include eyelashes on a human eyelid, and the brain with all its wondrous functions? How about all the microscopic organisms, all functions of the human body, the placement of the sun, moon, stars, the seasons and all their reasons for being? O, my, let's not forget the planets. There is still plenty of searching to be done, isn't there?

Let's put the Big Bang into perspective. It is still in its infancy and fizzles in comparison with the spiritual—God. It is His creation. And I guarantee He never gave it over to chance. If there was a Big Bang, God was the spark and the Creator. All we have to do is to look around and study our history. The Big Bang wouldn't exist unless it was part of God's Master Plan. Just as everything else that exists is part of His Master Plan, from the greatest to the minutest. The Big Bang has been around for years and it is still being studied, and apparently, some are still refuting it. What does that say about its credibility? Like all things unproven—the Hereafter, life after death, and creation remain mysteries. But, are they simply mysteries of chance? I assure you, I have more faith in life after death and the Hereafter than I do in the Big Bang Theory. I find it to be, in many ways, absurd. Its finite conclusions are still in a genesis stage. What most humans, including brilliant scientists, fail to recognize is that God will only give us what He believes we need.

He will not turn us into Himself, but He will give us what He knows will lead us to some of the answers we seek.

I have been accused of not believing in the scientific world and scientists who study and research and move forward in their lifelong searching and endeavors. Au contraire! I do not find their work to be worthless, but endless. It involves a very small intellectual community of great understanding and insight, which is further diminished when compared with the great whole—worlds beyond our own—God's world. Will humanity ever find all the answers it seeks regarding the beginning—our beginning? Question—"What beginning, the beginning of the unknown at large, which surely must include "our beginning?" Should it not? I wish all scientists Godspeed and success, but I hold fast to my belief that God exists and is the keeper of the answers scientists and researchers will seek ad infinitum. They are trying to access "God's Brain." Now that's a challenge. Isn't it? And, I would be as tenacious as they, if I were in their circle of work and discovery. And further, I am not denying their belief in God, or that they feel He does not exist. I simply feel that they question His existence too frequently. What some scientists forget is what they have never created. Theirs is the world of discovery, not necessarily creation. Who among them has created anything in God's world?

Actually, the only difference between their thinking and mine, I believe and accept God as sole Creator. Without a doubt, I accept His Master Plan. His power splits the atoms and makes their beginnings continue to evolve. We after all are a very minute part of the whole that exists beyond our knowledge and understanding. So, the only way I can believe in the Big Bang and other theories about our beginning and creation is to recognize the Creator as God. I am not denying scientists, or their wonderful work. After all, where would we be without them? I am simply recording my belief that—everything begins and ends as it began. We are not in charge. We only think we are. And, if we did not continue to question, research, and move forward, we would reach the end. Would we not? God is not searching, we are. But, there is another critical aspect to "the end," and that is time. Exactly where does time fit into the beginning and creation?

If I am privileged to meet my Maker, the first question that I would like to ask Him is—"Since time is yours and yours alone, how long is long in your Heavenly home?" We seem to define time and claim it for our own. However, I recognize that time belongs to God. That's why life has no guarantee. If it did, most would opt to live forever as we are now. We give little thought to time, and rarely think throughout life about the fact that,

"With the seed of life, comes the seed of death . . ."
That's irrefutable.
"And with the seed of death, comes a new seed of
life . . . a new beginning . . ."
That's one of my beliefs.

That has a great deal to do with my philosophy of the Hereafter and Our Next Assignment, Our Next Grand Adventure.

Before I move on, I must mention another of my beliefs, that of angels. Why should I believe in their existence as I do? Because I believe they are a part of life and life after death. They are the spirits that guide and hold us close in life, and they are the stars in the heavens. Therefore, I embrace them all. Throughout my lifetime, I have been privileged to be faithfully supported and strengthened in my many times of need. To not mention them would be an oversight that would haunt me. How I wish that I could acknowledge each of them individually. Extend with deep gratitude and warm love my thanks.

They are not only heavenly spirits, but live in the flesh. Don't ever dismiss the fact that angels walk with you every day. They are part of your earthly life. Can anyone among you deny their presence in your life? Have you ever served as an angel? I don't know if I ever have, but I would hope that to be so.

Angels mine, wherever you are I know that you are with me, and have been for my lifetime. I will always be indebted to you for your concern and love. Stay close. I look forward to meeting with you in my afterlife.

"OH!"

“OH!”

“OH, GOD!”

"I JUST DIED"

Veil of the Heavenly Mist

"What Do I Do Now?"

I haven't a clue. I wish someone would tell me. I have been vaporized. I am but a spirit on the move. But, the question is, "Am I moving?" I really can't say. I simply feel as though I am floating in the "Veil of the Heavenly Mist." However, my mind seems to be functioning. Is that possible? I feel as though I am thinking out loud. Whatever happened to reality? Or, is this the "ultimate" reality? I have never known such silence and peace. Yet, I sense anxiety. How can that be? Perhaps it is my eagerness to join my Maker and those with whom I lived and laughed on Earth.

It's quite quiet—not a sound. The air is pleasant. It is cool and fresh, and since I am not in control, I guess I will just have to wait for help. But, I do wonder whether I will walk on a staircase or be jet-propelled to the "Pearly Gates."

Oops! I am standing on a staircase. It is a very strange staircase. It is made up of hands, but whose?

Oh, my, look, they are labeled. They are the hands of those who helped me along life's way. My family, all my friends, church and business associates, they were angels all. It is quite a list, all those people, all those helping hands and all those steps. This is going to take a while. But, I'm on my way. Step-by-step, hand-by-hand, I am moving very slowly, but I am being elevated. "Phew," that's good. At least for now I am going in the right direction.

This is really very peculiar. Every now and again, there are long pauses, and gaps in the staircase. I guess I am being given time to reflect, time to think about my life and how I lived it. But for some reason, my thoughts are still reverting back to life and death, the Hereafter, and my Heavenly home. The thoughts that I wished to share with everyone while living, but somehow I never did. Now in death, my final state of repose, I will share them with all who will listen. This is so exciting. I am travelling back to my Heavenly home to be with those I knew all my life. But, before I begin my exposé and expound upon my thoughts and beliefs, I must share the things that brought me to them. The breaks in the staircase will afford me that precious time to tell you what I never could while living. Tell you about the Hereafter, my Heavenly home, I hope." Please, whoever is in charge, don't turn me away.

Now, what do I want to say about the Hereafter? Well, my first thoughts, my very early thoughts were about life and death. They were challenging. I still remember them well, and apparently others do too, otherwise, why would there be gaps in the staircase? I still feel as I have said before, that I am being given time to remember, evaluate, and share.

Thoughts—my thoughts, my very early thoughts. Believe me, I am pressed to share them now, before it is too late, and I lose my last opportunity to do so.

This is what I believe. In the beginning, there is life. In the beginning, there is death. The old state of being dies to let the new state of being begin. Death has a beginning, just as it counterpart, life.

But to accept death, one must give up the question, "In death, do we find a new beginning?" The answer for me is, "Yes." We must begin by accepting life and death as being one. For with the seed of life, comes the seed of death. My belief is that the transformation of one, leads into the emergence of the other. And, with the seed of death, comes the seed of life.

We never die. ***We are Life Everlasting.***

We live and wait to be called through death into Our Next Assignment, Our Next Grand Adventure. I have given this much thought, and I have come to the conclusion that it is logical.

I have been haunted most of my life with thoughts on life, and death, and the Hereafter. And, I have asked myself many times, where, oh, where, did it all begin? Why should I even ask? For I know where. I lived it. It all began when I was a child.

It began when my father passed away right in front of me, as quickly as any breath, when I was all of five years of age. And given my age, no one believed that I would remember the incident. However, I did. And throughout my life, with each death that occurred, the memories returned. I always pushed them aside, but they were never really "buried." Life in that instant had changed me forever. And as I grew and matured, more and more questions without answers became apparent. I really never found anyone who had any answers to satisfy my interest and curiosity about what happens after we die. It seemed as though I was never going to finish my quest.

But now that I have joined the land of those who have the answers, I will fill in those blanks and confirm my belief.

For a lifetime, everyone including my family suggested that I just forget my inquiries about life, death, and the Hereafter. Advice, skip it. Chalk it up to morbid curiosity. Let it go. But, I couldn't. I had to know. Do we simply go away and remain in the dirt forever? Even theologians could not answer me. When some tried to satisfy my questions, it seemed as though they were all reading from the same manuscript. It was handwritten and waiting to be changed, if not corrected.

Finally, several Bibles gave me the ultimate answer. After reading, and reading, and reading, I found what I was looking for. As noted in the Chapter I, God defines the Hereafter through his Son. Think about *Jesus' words,*

"Do not let your heart be troubled. Trust in God; trust also in me. In my Father's house are MANY ROOMS; if it were not so, I would have told you. I am going there to prepare a place for you. And if I go and prepare a place for you, I will come back and take you to be with me that you also may be where I am. You know the way to the place where I am going." John 14:1-4 (NIV-New International Version). And as I searched further and delved into several Bibles, the "rooms" in God's house, varied, based upon each edition.

> ***. . . "In my Father's house there are MANY DWELLING PLACES." . . . John 14:2 (NRSV-New Revised Standard Version) and (TNAB-New American Bible, St. Joseph Edition)***
>
> ***. . . "In my Father's house there are MANY ROOMS." . . . John 14:2 (RSV-Revised Standard Version)***
>
> ***. . . "In my Father's house are many MANSIONS: . . ." John 14:2 (KJV-King James Version)***
>
> ***"And as Jesus hung on the cross with a thief on each side, one said, "Jesus, remember me when you come into your kingdom." Jesus answered him, "I tell you the truth, today you will be with me in paradise." Luke 23:42-43 (NIV-New International Version)***

No matter the Bible, or the minor differences, they all deliver the same message. To truly know life and death is all a matter of faith and belief. "The Promise" above is real, and my message taps its core. There is plenty of space forever for all. Of this I am sure. Our Heavenly home has a beginning, but no end. Our Creator's qualities of Omnipotence and Omnipresence define life, and death, and everlasting.

I really can't pinpoint to the second, when I latched onto this unending quest for a Hereafter answer. Nor can I ever count, or understand, the aggregate of faithful who doubt "life after death." I just listen in amazement. And just think, this is simply one of millions of topics that are challenged in the "*Good Book*." Perhaps it was written to be challenged—to expand our minds—to make us truly understand its contents.

One of the most frequent comments regarding our spirits rising and life after death, life everlasting, concerns our final resting place in our home in the Hereafter. Time and time again, I have been challenged to explain how so many people could have passed away and found a place in God's house of many rooms. "There aren't enough rooms, never could be, or will be." Many people, trying to satisfy their doubt have converted the house of many rooms into a "mansion" with many rooms. Literally speaking, that doesn't make sense, that thinking is flawed also. And to support and defend that creation, they argue, "Just think about all the people who have lived and died since the beginning of time. It is impossible for that many rooms to exist in Heaven." So, they increased the size of the house to a mansion. Hey, folks, it's still too small.

No. The rooms do exist. They are here. I can see them as I move on the staircase in my new spiritual state. And I know exactly what they are. I will define "the rooms" for you later.

Before long I will reveal where my faith journey has brought me. I am secure in my belief. I know where I am going and why. I will share my theory with you, without reservation. And hopefully, give you a comfort for your own everlasting life, one that reaches far beyond your "final" resting place, your dirt bed, your ashes in an urn.

But let it be known, before I died and found myself in the place where I am now, my search had always carried me to the heavens, the sky, the vastness of space, the planets, the stars, the universe(s) however many. No need to doubt the Son of God's words. There is plenty of room, once you let go of the mansions and the human concept of many rooms. Let your thoughts stretch into a proper realm of logic. As I have said before, I believe my theory is logical, but I anticipate that it will be refuted and scoffed at. And I submit, all who choose to do so, probably will have no explanation or answer, beyond my thoughts, my premise. I am hopeful too, that I may even help others find comfort in their search for everlasting rest and peace. But for now, suffice it to say, "We never die. We are life everlasting." Be comforted. We should never limit ourselves. After all, aren't our limitations based solely on our human knowledge and abilities? Doesn't "human" say it all?

It does for me. So, to be fair to yourself, ask yourself, "Do I believe in the Hereafter? Why?" Some people do not. They know they will die and be relegated forever to their dirt bed. The end! How shallow their tomorrow. No deeper than the grave itself.

I cannot bring myself to believe that my spirit, my life, will be buried forever with my flesh and bones which will eventually disappear. It has to be more precious than that to my Creator. Why proverbially speaking, even in cliché terms, "reinvent the wheel." If it rolls, is it not good? It has had life and spirit. Why should my life, my spirit be defunct? Why should my character, my feelings, my soul, be gone forever, after all my years of learning, doing, creating who I am? There has to be some value, a value for another tomorrow and beyond.

Yes, there are some faiths that believe you will be held accountable in the Hereafter for your life actions on earth. As noted, others believe once you pass away, that's it. Does either of these thoughts define your thoughts? Live in the present, as you will. If you do well, will that satisfy you, you alone, your conscience, your Creator? Is there any striving for tomorrow and Eternal life in that thinking, or is it just for today. It is for now, and only now.

My belief is different. We not only live life in this life, but one or more beyond it. That is for me the meaning of "Life Everlasting."

Given that, and my present spiritual state, travelling on a hand-staircase in the Hereafter, "What should I say to you now? Welcome to eternity."

You did not know it at the time, but the "Veil of the Heavenly Mist" page that you walked through with me earlier, actually was my introduction to Heaven. It represented my initial cross-over journey from living to spirit. I walked into the "Veil of the Unknown—to begin my new life in the Hereafter." The world in which theories and speculations abound, run rampant. Why not define the Hereafter as you envision it? What do you want? What do you expect? Or, do you simply embrace and advocate what others have created for you? As I have suggested, redefine the Hereafter for yourself, so that it becomes part of you, your spirit. That is what I did. I defined it for myself.

I am the only one who decided where I am going and why. And I invite you to join me. Come keep me company, while I tell a story about the great beyond. At some later date, I hope that I will be able to talk to God about His creations, and respectfully offer some recommendations for changes in the development of future generations.

Are you curious yet? I hope so, because the following words and thoughts represent my theories, my beliefs, and my understanding of our tomorrow. I have found a place for me in God's mansion of many rooms, and I have found one for each of you also. I know what the rooms are and where they are, and I know that there are never-ending places for all who believe in and expect to reside in God's Heavenly home, the Hereafter. Yes, there are "rooms" for people of all faiths. What we have not accomplished on earth, we will in Heaven and on subsequent Assignments. There will be a gentle, quiet, everlasting PEACE, not as you know it now, but more beautiful in a new world. It is not an end, but a beginning. We will live as the title says in the Hereafter, and eventually be given Our Next Assignment, Our Next Grand Adventure.

Do you think that we will live in a Crypt of Forever sealed forever? Or, is it only sealed to block our return to earth, and keep the mystery of life after death a mystery? Well then, think about this. Should we return, who will know us, when all who knew us, are gone? Is that logical?

For me the best and only earthly place to bury a loved one is not in a cemetery or a mausoleum, but in the heart. After all, they are locked with love in the crypt of the mind anyway. Memories good and bad always rise to the surface. Always find their way into our world of REMEMBER. Remember this? Remember that? Remember when? Remember who? Remember why? I wonder if all those who were involved in my life, those who took part in each memory, still care. Will they queue up to greet me upon my arrival in the Hereafter? Will they? And, will they say, as I will in the future to you, "Welcome to Eternity?"

I know that I am headed to an historical Eternity to begin again. But, over the course of my lifetime, I did consider "Who am I, and how did I become who I am and was? What combination of cells came together to form me? Were they not all part of my spirit? And did they not remain part of my spirit in death?"

After all, all babies are born different in the flesh, the genes. Won't they be part of my body in death? How far back do genes go? How about back to the beginning of time. They would have to, wouldn't they? So then, whose genes are floating in your body—in mine? Our mother's, our father's, our grandmother's, our grandfather's, great-grandmother's, great-grandfather's, great-great-great-great-great, etc.—Adam's and Eve's, or prior—those of the universe before and beyond? Who knows? Do I? Perhaps. Now that's potpourri. It comes from a French word meaning: "Rotten Pot." Ouch! Sorry I mentioned it.

But what am I basing that "perhaps" upon? I am now entering the world of what might number quadrillions of speculators, believing their answers to be "the correct answers" to the age-old question, "Where do we go when we die?"

Well, that question I am sure has been rattling around since the beginning of time. And the most frequently expressed answer to the query is, "who knows?" No one has come back to tell us. Have they?" Are we sure no one has come back? Just as the mystery itself has survived, did the mystery of those who may have given an answer go unheard? Were we listening? Is it something beautiful and obvious? Did someone speak to me so that I could share what I am sharing with you—so that I could espouse my belief? I often wonder, why? Why did I withhold my belief and theory for such a long time, and why did I constantly over that time question me. Why do I feel as I do? Did I alone come up with these thoughts, originate these ideas? Before I left my good earth, I did a lot of writing and I always felt as though someone or something was giving me the words, giving me the thoughts. O, that inner muse—that inner spirit that "snuck" into my brain and latched on to its waves. Theologians have forever pondered the answer to "the question." They share what they believe to be true, when satisfying those in need of a definitive answer, an answer to ease their fears of the unknown, their fears about life after death.

In that scenario, when I was alive, I realized that we surely must question the strength of everyone's faith. And also, I must question my own. I pondered the questions, do I fear death? I don't know. Will I fear death, when it comes my way? I can only pray that I will not. Certainly I don't want to. But I did want to know what rumbled through the minds of those who were headed to the Hereafter from the beginning of that journey until the end, and then, move with them one step further beyond the beginning of the end. Will I find it to be an end, making room for a new, unknown, yet to be seen beginning? Obviously, I believe wholeheartedly in beginnings. I believe that my final goodbye is only temporary. For as long as you believe in life, whether ***earthly*** or ***eternal***, you will live. For life is everlasting. Now I am dead, I no longer have to answer those questions.

Our beginning is actually the beginning of our end. As I recall, many times writers envision life as being lived on a stage. And at the end, when we are filled with fear, the curtain either does not rise, or it closes without encores. That's an interesting metaphor. But I wonder why they never write about whether the same degree of the fear of dying exists before birth? After birth, the curtain parts, is that when we begin acting out our lives on earth's stage according to a script? We know the Creator, but what is the name of the play? Is it entitled by my birth name, or the family applied ***nom de plume***? Is it a comedy? Is it a tragedy? Will it be in the end, a mystery? Hmmmm. Isn't life a compilation of all the aforementioned—the rise and fall of our own personal empires?

Other than in our infancy, do we not choose the characters with whom we wish to act, share, and place on our stages, until the curtain closes or falls? It is strange how the fear of death steals our stage in the end. None of us ever closes the curtain by choice, and rarely if ever, as we would like—without an encore. Could our wake represent our final curtain call? Or, would that be our Creator's final creation for us? The question is, "Will we be stepping unto another stage to begin a new career?" I believe we will. Could that explain why so many who have had a death experience mention a bright light? Could it simply be the footlights of a new life? Certainly that would explain Life Everlasting, life without end. That's probably why some acts are more enjoyable and memorable than others, and some music is more haunting and hummable than others. The show must go on. And life then would live on. Where does that leave me? Where should I begin, life before birth or life after death? Will it be Everlasting? Eternal? What do you think? I will soon find out for I am on my way to my Eternal tomorrow.

Oops! I am stalled. The staircase has stopped. But, my mind has not.

I am sure now that each one of these interruptions in my journey is definitely and specifically planned. They have a purpose. Could it actually represent Hell? Each stop lengthens and delays my journey to where I want to be. This could be my ***IMMORTAL CONSCIENCE*** reviewing, and reviewing, and reviewing my real life. My conscious and subconscious joining forces to somehow justify my life long thoughts and actions, my right and wrong decisions. Again, could this time be my time in Purgatory or Hell? Is my transitional trip to Heaven paved with Hell time?

An ***IMMORTAL CONSCIENCE***—Is it a final review of how we thought about "life and death?"

Obviously, there are many ways to look at life. I know what I believe and that belief is based on the strongest of powers in action, God in Creation mode. It all begins with an act of God. No, nothing, nothing is beyond the mind and hand of the spirit in and about that which controls everything that exists. I maintain, like all those who create in life, it is most difficult to share, sell, or give away any creation. For, it is part of the creator forever.

If we think about the human body, and all its wonders, who would want to permanently destroy it? Think about all the time and effort it took to put it together, to make it work. We did not create human beings, humanity, so it is rather easy for us to dispose of it without thought, or pain. Whoever said "life is cheap. It has no value." They defined it in human terms. And, who destroys more of humanity than humanity? Let us face it. How can there be perpetual life, without perpetual people? Is that possible? And what are perpetual people—spirits, the spirits of the past who remain in memory only?

I often feel the spirits of the past. They are close, yet so far away. I can see their faces, their eyes, but I cannot hear their voices. That void of silence is dark, deep and disheartening. On the weekends, how I longed for the telephone to ring and hear the laughter of my two oldest and dearest friends, now gone for many years. We would giggle over nothing and be too serious about things that were not that serious at all. That's life, in a time and a place. Time and place, life and history move on. But be it recognized and known, time belongs to God**.** Will time be forever? Who knows?—Only its rightful owner. Well, let's get back to life. I believed that life is prescheduled, not predestined. You are given a time to be born and a time to die. That's why there is no guarantee. Only God handles time. We live and die by His clock, not ours. And in between, we live out life's schedule. Paths cross with those we are scheduled to meet.

Some are scheduled to marry and have children, others not. We are scheduled to attend school and reach predetermined levels of academic achievement. We are scheduled to rent an apartment, buy a house, work at a specific job, and meet specific people. Everything has and is on a life schedule. And, we are scheduled to return from whence we came.

This is not a predestination theory, because we can choose, make choices. We have been given a Will. It's God given, given to be used. I don't believe we are predestined to meet certain people and stay with them. We meet, we greet, and we can by our own choice by Will, move on. Question is, will we be judged on our achievements and the performance of our predetermined opportunities and feats? Did we accept and fulfill the feats? We had to choose. Which did we turn down, and how did we complete that phase of our lives? How did we fill that void? Everything was prescheduled and then, within that scenario, we had to accept or deny that part of our life, the part where decisions in the making came into effect. Our Will was set into motion. If it was predestined, we would have no control. Wouldn't we ask, are we then really in charge? My God, who is in charge?

How would that thought make us feel? To have a far superior power, an alter-ego, direct our every move, our show for life. To have it be part of a Predestined Plan. We would be the same as everything else in our lives. Just as the seasons fall into place and occur on schedule, and the tide moves in ebb and flow, and the wind blows and subsides, the flowers bloom on cue and the rain turns to snow. Just as a leopard cannot change its spots and stars cannot be seen in daylight with the "naked eye." Whoa, who really is in charge? We have a Will. Question is, "How do we use it?" Or in my case now, "How did I use it?"

Oops! The staircase is moving again.

Good! That means I will have more time to tell you about my three closest friends. I expected them to meet me. I thought that they would be here already. But then again, I really haven't arrived at my final destination, and they could be on their Next Assignments, their Next Grand Adventures. I will just have to be more patient. I will just have to cool my jets.

But I am anxious. Time is short. So, I must begin this lengthy story before my time on the staircase runs out. Also, I need time to tell you where you will be going after death, and where your Hereafter home is located. But before I do that, you and I must go on a ***"Fantastic Journey."***

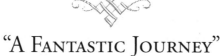

"A Fantastic Journey"

"WHERE WERE YOU LAST NIGHT?"

The sky was ablaze with vivid colors as their hues danced among the hundreds of stars, planetary moons, asteroids, and comets that floated and darted in all directions against the dark multi-colored universal background. And there I was a lonely traveler taking in the sites. Come journey with me and share my experience. Learn about my epiphany, which surely will someday be yours also

Jeanette Dowdell,

Let me tell you about my friends, Merc, Jupe and Veni. They had been friends for many years, in fact, inseparable. Strange names? Yes, but they were very proud of them. Obviously, they each were nicknamed for a planet . . . Merc was named after the planet Mercury . . . Jupe for Jupiter and Veni for Venus. They were so named because of their physical characteristics and their personalities. The reasons will be clarified as the story evolves.

It actually all began when they decided to meet and have a friendly get-together. It had been far too long between visits. However, their "get-together" suddenly turned into something none had expected it to be. When Merc telephoned Jupe to confirm the time of their visit, it sounded as though there was an emergency. According to him, Jupe apparently was in some sort of trouble. So the plan was that they would hold a "chew the fat . . ." session to discuss whatever the problem was. The simple get-together had changed. According to Veni, when Merc called her, he said that Jupe was looking for more than simply moral support. Jupe told him that he had a very strange tale to relate. He had experienced an out-of-body journey overnight. He was still spooked and reeling. Obviously, Veni's and Merc's curiosity was beyond peaked. Merc, in addition to hearing about Jupe's journey, really wanted to question him about why he had not shown up for a large gathering of friends the prior night and without even asking, he was about to find out. Everyone was concerned about Jupe, asking, "Where is he, why is he among the missing?" No one could reach him by telephone, on his ipad or blackberry, etc. And, that was totally out of character for Jupe. Now, knowing all of this, Merc called for Veni and they drove to Jupe's place. When they arrived and Jupe answered the door, they were both surprised at how he looked and acted. He was pale and quite shaken. "Come in and sit down. Thanks for coming." Jokes were definitely not in order. But, one question was, and Merc in order to get the conversation started, said,

"Hey Jupe, 'Where were you last night?'"

"Who wants to know?"

Merc said, "I do."

"And, who are you?"

"Very funny, my friend . . . you know that we were supposed to meet at Jimmy's last night, and you didn't show up. *Gallactia* was particularly upset. She had planned a surprise for you, and she was very disappointed."

Veni piped up to say, "We all were surprised."

"Thanks, Veni."

"Merc continued, "Are you still swoonin' over *Gallactia*?"

"You bet! She is the greatest . . . very special"

"Jupe, "Where were you last night?"

"First, Merc, tell me how *Gallactia* got her name. I know you know."

Merc responded quickly, "Her mother made it up. She always dreamed of having a little girl who would someday become a star. Jupe, "Stop changing the subject." Enough about that; no more stalling, 'Where were you last night?'"

"You're right my friends, I'm stalling. I'm afraid to tell you, where I was last night, because you probably won't believe me."

"Try us, Jupe."

"Okay. I took a trip."

"Oh, yeah, where did you go?"

"Out of this world . . . I journeyed far beyond the earth and sped throughout the Universe. I saw and heard things that most people have never seen, or heard. I can't explain how it happened, or how I am now sitting here ready to tell you about my fantastic voyage. And believe me, it was fantastic.

"Hey Jupe, have you been drinking or somethin'?"

"No. I am quite sober and very calm now, although I wasn't early this morning. I kept checking to see if I was still flesh and blood—and in my own body.

"What do you mean by that?"

All Jupe could see, as Merc asked the question, were Veni and Merc with giant eyes and dropped-open mouths. There was no need for any more questions. The eyes said it all. What Jupe intuitively knew was that his friends were mentally saying, "Are you for real? Are you crazy? Have you flipped?" However, there was no sound, simply a stunned silence. Jupe knew he definitely scared the bejeesus out of his friends. Veni's and Merc's eyes were transfixed, as well as their mouths. So, in order to break the dead silence, Jupe went right on telling the story of his wonderful journey.

"Are you ready for this, my friends?

"Yes, of course."

"Try not to look at me like that. I really don't know how it all happened. Without warning, part of me left my body. It was as if life itself had been sucked out and transported through the opened window and into the heavens. I was traveling without a space suit, or a backpack, or oxygen, or any life-support systems. I was traveling in a foreign gaseous state."

"What do you mean gaseous state?"

"Well, I really don't know. I don't know how to define it. Before I go on however, I need a glass of water."

"I think that you better get us one also, or something stronger. Thanks."

Veni and Merc sat opposite Jupe as he began to speak again. It was as if Jupe was running a race with himself; as if he didn't want to forget anything. Neither Veni nor Merc dared to interrupt, even though they desperately wanted to say, "Hey, stop."

Without flinching, Jupe said, "Once I left the atmosphere, I didn't know whether I was being propelled by an invisible supernatural force, or pulled by the gravitational forces of the outer world around me. Remarkably, at that moment, I was not scared, or worried, or even thinking about the situation. I felt as though I belonged. I guess the beauty that surrounded me was far too awesome, to bring me back to human thoughts. I was flying; flying in an endless cavern of sparkling gems that were pulsating and alive."

At this point, Jupe's eyes seemed to be twice their normal size. And when he took a breath, Merc seized the moment.

"Wait a minute, Jupe, I don't understand. What really happened? Exactly what are you telling us?"

"I can't explain it. But please, please, try to put yourselves in my place. How would you like to journey through space knowing that you were traveling in and through areas of extreme cold and heat and you couldn't feel any of its effects? How would you like to see your own galaxies with their billions of dim and bright stars dancing all around you; with their nebulae and supernova in action? How would you two like to take a journey like that?"

Merc and Veni said, almost in the same breath, "I don't know. To do what you did, might be great, but I would have to have some assurances that I would get back, before I died of fright."

"Don't be silly. I tell you, it was like diving deep into the sea; just you, all alone, traveling in a soundless atmosphere. Even breathing wasn't a problem. Instead of water, it was the heavens and rarefied air filled with sparkling diamond inhabitants, stars of all shapes and sizes. And I will tell you this; the intensity of their overwhelming brilliance would have captured your souls, just as they did mine. The stars appeared to be speaking a silent language; one that was theirs alone . . . the language of all those who occupied the heavens. And there I was taking it all in, while being unable to hear, or understand. I had no arms to reach out and touch those magnificent "twinklers." But all I kept thinking was, if only I could. I'm telling you, the lights, the colors, the contrasts were thousands of times more vivid than those on earth and they were brilliantly set against the blacks, the purples, the blues, the magentas and the violets of the grand heavenly expanse before me."

Merc and Veni suddenly realized that with every breath, Jupe was leaving them, traveling farther away from 'Mother Earth' and into the realms of the heavenly deep again, even though he was sitting on the couch in his own living room. At one point during his verbal marathon, Jupe suddenly stopped and said, "I used to think that the stars formed galaxies, even though I read the opposite was true. Now, I know firsthand that galaxies form stars, and they put on quite a show. My age old question was not which came first, 'the chicken or the egg?' It was always, 'the star or the galaxy?'" I knew what the scientists had revealed to us, but now I know without question, because of what I saw. I also learned that the stars are Earth's remembered and forgotten. I'll explain that to both of you later, when I feel you are ready for that explanation."

Following those remarks, Jupe slipped into some form of trance and quietly drifted far away.

As they looked at Jupe, they couldn't say that they weren't somewhat unhinged by his story. In fact, they began to mentally revisit what stars and galaxies were all about. They began testing their own knowledge. What are stars? Where do they come from? Are they hot, or cold? Are they colorless? Are they actually alive, as Jupe had just alluded to? And if so, how long do they live? WOW! It's endless and only a miniscule part of the whole. There is so much more to be discovered, and it always amazed them how humans fail to recognize and consider their place in it. Nevertheless, they sat quiet, but very anxious for Jupe to continue. However, Jupe would first have to return to them in their space and time.

Since Merc and Veni were both teachers, an in-depth conversation began. How much did they actually remember about the stars? They should have been telling Jupe this story, not he telling them. But for them, it was a regression. They both had moved on to bigger and better space events. They left others to delve into the stars. Come to think of it, Merc and Veni had been working lately almost exclusively on planetary exploration.

But STARS they both agreed were their all-time favorite subject. When Merc and Veni pulled together in their younger years, they recalled how they went running around asking everyone tons of questions about the stars. How naïve they were. They actually asked a NASA employee, "What are stars?"

And according to them, he was patient and kind. As they recalled, he simply filled in the blanks; a lot of them. He went on to say, "Well, they are actually bodies of hot glowing gas that vary greatly in size, mass and temperature. Temperatures can range from 5,500° F to 90,000° F and their diameters can be anywhere from 450 times smaller to 1,000 times larger than the *SUN*. And the strangest thing is that the hottest stars are *BLUE*; the coolest are *RED*. Wouldn't you think that the opposite to be true? Stars are born in *NEBULAE*. And, "What are they, we said?" Well, a *NEBULA* is a cloud of *DUST* and *GAS* inside a *GALAXY*.

I remembered how Merc and Veni commented at that time about the fact that humans were dust and gas. And from that time on, I always thought that there was a peculiar allegorical comparison between stars and humans. For example: Reflection Nebulae shine because their dust reflects light in and around the nebulae where the stars are born. Now, how many humans shine, grow, and succeed, because of their environments—the people and things around them in their lifetimes?

Dark Nebulae, on the other hand, appear as silhouettes because they block light from shining nebulae or stars behind them. Think about that. How many people do not succeed because of their inescapable lifelong environments—the actions of other human beings and roadblocks placed before them? Interesting isn't it? You might just say that they are born dying stars.

A Planetary Nebulae—a gas shell drifting away from a dying stellar core is like a core of human deadbeats, who hold tight to someone who should have been given wings and flight. And then of course, the Supernova Remnant, the gas shell moving away at great speed from a stellar core, after a violent explosion (Supernova), which compares to a the group of special humans who had been given knowledge, exposure and love to go forth with hope and dreams of becoming a star.

O, my, now I'm getting carried away. This is their story.

All of a sudden, Jupe seems slowly to be coming alive again.

"Hi, Jupe."

"Hey guys, 'Where have I been?'"

"Oh, I guess you are still tired from your journey."

"And, 'What were you doing, while I was drifting?'"

"You wouldn't believe it, Jupe, but we were reviewing our old days, our knowledge about the stars, because we wanted to be prepared for the rest of your journey. But, you came back too soon. We never got to the full galaxies and the planets."

"Hey guys, where did I leave off?"

"You left off by saying something about the stars being Earth's remembered and forgotten. And we sure want to hear more about that."

"Oh, you will later. In the meantime, I want to talk to you about our Milky Way. It's wonderful and I can't just do a flash fly-by. Not with my teacher buddies sitting here.

To us Earthlings, the Milky Way is just a faint band of light that stretches across the night sky, but get up close and you see that the light comes from stars and nebulae in our galaxy. Sometimes it's simply called "The Galaxy." It's shaped like a spiral, with a dense central bulge that is encircled by four arms spiraling outward and surrounded by a less halo. The central bulge is a small, dense sphere that contains mainly older red and yellow stars. The halo is a less dense region in which the oldest stars are situated; some of the stars may be as old as the Galaxy itself—some 15 billion years old. The spiral arms contain mainly hot, young, blue stars, as well as nebulae. You know the clouds of dust and gas, inside which stars are born.

Veni, Merc, 'The Galaxy' is vast—about 100,000 light-years across (a light-year is about 5,879 billion miles); in comparison, the Solar System seems small, at about 12 light-hours across (about 8 billion miles). The entire Galaxy is just sitting there rotating in space, with the inner stars traveling faster than those further out. I was there for a while, I'm sure. It was wonderful to see and again, the colors were divine. The most startling tidbit coming out of that visitation was the fact that the Sun, which is about two-thirds out from the center, completes one lap of the Galaxy about every 220 million years. Just think about that.

"Jupe, you make the whole thing sound so exciting."

"Oh, my God it was. I didn't know how fast, or slow, I was traveling, or if my speed varied depending upon where I was. The only thing that I knew for certain was that it didn't bother me. I was not nervous or frightened by the whole experience, until I recognized what was the former planet, "Pluto."

"Hey, how did you know the planet, Pluto?"

"It barked at me."

"Very funny!"

"I remember reading a book about the planets a long time ago, when we all were studying about the universe in class, and I specifically remembered something about Pluto . . . its moon, Charon. It was half the size of its parent planet, and because of that, they were sometimes considered to be a double-planet system. Small planet, large moon, how could I have missed it? When I got home, out of sheer curiosity, I checked Pluto's diameter. It only measures 1,429 miles and it was then recognized as one of our outermost planets. Today, it's not. It is now classified as a "Dwarf Planet." However, when I saw Pluto and Charon face-to-face, that's when I winced. I guess, I realized how far from home I actually had come. Here's an update, an interesting point. Today, we now know that there are a very large number of small objects in the KUIPER BELT beyond the orbit of Neptune. I didn't see them, but they are roughly the same size as Pluto. I can't wait for more news about that.

Listen, I've got to stop again for a while. I'm getting hungry. Would you like to have something to eat and drink?"

"Merc piped up and said, "Okay." You know me. There's always room for food. I haven't changed much since we graduated high school."

"Oh, my God, don't say that. That was eons ago. That was where we all got our "classy names."""

"Hey, you're right. Yeah, and strangely enough, it had something to do with the planets we were studying at that time. Weren't we lucky, and crazy?"

"Let's see. As I recall, back then, I was much bigger than you. I had a bit of a stormy temper, more 'spacey' and didn't bother to control my gas emissions; typical teenager. But, I was very fast for my size, so they named me "Jupe," after the planet, Jupiter, which is much further away from Earth than Mercury. Oh, yeah, you on the other hand, were smaller in stature, ironed willed and much faster than I. So they named you, "Merc," after the planet, Mercury with its iron core and a speed of 30 miles per second; 1,800 miles per minute. You were 'hot stuff;' closest to the Sun, while I on the other hand, was floating in the fifth orbit around the Sun. How strange. We were miles apart in space, yet, the best of friends in our Earthly confines." And you, Veni, were and still are beautiful. You were identified with the Greek goddess Aphrodite, and the Roman Mythological goddess of love. To say nothing of the fact that Venus the planet is the brightest, sixth largest planet in the solar system and second in distance from the sun. Hot stuff! Let me be frank, and offer a gentle comment . . . we're still "space cadets."

"They were good days, weren't they? Hey, what's on the menu?"

"How would you like a ham or bacon and egg sandwich?" Merc? Veni?

"That sounds good to me" . . . "me too." But you better keep talking, while you take on the role of short-order cook. This story sounds like it is going to take a bit of time in the tellin'. And, don't burn anything."

Veni yelled, "If ya need help, gimme a shout."

"Merc, are you still giving orders? Any more boss? Some things never change."

"Come on, Jupe, tell us more."

"Where did I leave off?"

"You left off with the barking Pluto. You were wincing."

"Right! I knew that I had counted eight other orbiting planetary bodies. Each one was majestic in its own right. I remembered certain physically observable characteristics about them as I passed. I also remembered being distracted by an inexplicable prodding, as I moved. I was being injected with knowledge; information by osmosis. Something was repeating over and over, 'Absorb what you see, hear, and feel.' Suddenly, I realized that Pluto was at the end of our Solar System, as we knew it then. Haven't times changed? I didn't only wince, I wanted to recoil, but couldn't. I just wanted to go home. Tell me true, wouldn't you two?"

"Of course."

"I have to tell you, even in my gaseous state, I felt something very human. Even though I said before that I was not frightened, I had a slight sensation of uneasiness. All I kept thinking, beyond my intrigue, was, "Why am I here? Am I going to stop moving further and further away from my home?

Why is this happening to me? Who is in charge here? Where are the brakes?"

"What do you think guys?"

"Right now, we are afraid to tell you what we think. What do you think, we should think? What if we were you and you were listening to Veni or me? What would you think?

"Well, let's put it this way, you haven't run out to call the men in the white jackets yet. So, there is some hope. Would you really like me to continue?"

"Of course, this is beyond fantastic."

"The thing that bothered me the most, I really couldn't figure out how fast I was traveling. I kept asking myself, "Am I traveling at a *supersonic speed*, or are these visions coming to me one at a time in sequential order? It seemed to me that I was not only traveling at *supersonic speed*, but up or down a special path in order to see all the planets as they were situated in relation to the Sun.

Jupe forgot the food, as he once again sat down opposite Veni and Merc who were on the couch. He wanted to watch their reactions to his commentary. He studied their faces and body language and wondered whether or not, he should ask one of them to take notes. But on second thought, he decided against it for now . . . perhaps later. And so, on he went.

"I know that there had to be some sort of an adjustment made as I traveled because, logically, each planet was in its own elliptical orbit. Therefore, for me to see them in their proper planetary, sequential order, I had to zigzag or be moved to catch them just as they passed on my path. Another thing, time seemed to stand still. I was very aware of that, and very confused by the fact that I felt that I had reached Pluto in such a relatively short period of time. However for this trip, time played no part, it was irrelevant.

"What was that like?"

"What—the irrelevancy of time, seeing Pluto, or traveling at an accelerated rate?"

"All of them."

"Well, I knew that I had passed the other eight planets in our Solar System, because I saw some of their moons, asteroids, comets and meteorites, as I was dodging some foreign flying objects. Come to think of it, I did not have control over my movements, so they could have dodged me, while I thought that I was dodging them. I just can't say for certain. I do remember though, that the stomach I thought I had left behind, took a turn or two, when I was jettisoned toward the Sun and saw Neptune whiz by. Hey, Merc, 'How come, wise guy, you didn't ask me, "How did you know it was Neptune?'"

"Well, Jupe, before I do that, I must say, for someone who supposedly took a trip last night, you don't know very much about it, physically, do you?" Now, "How did you know that the planet was Neptune?"

"It had to be, because the next closest planet was, Pluto. And speaking of Pluto, did you know that it loses its outmost planet status when its elliptical orbit passes inside the orbit of Neptune? That happens every 20 years of its 248 year orbit around the Sun. Let me tell you, its gray, solid and icy surface is ugly, but it's a speedy little devil. With your love of speed, Merc, I had to mention that."

"My speed days are over. Go on."

"Imagine, if you can, that little Pluto ball traveling at thirty miles per second. That's 1800 miles per minute. It's as hot as hell on the sun-lit side—800° F and only—270° F on the dark side. "Which side would you prefer, Merc? Veni?"

"They both responded, "neither, Jupe," but this is surely bringing us back to stats and info that we thought we buried forever. Somehow, we both feel that you were always more into that stuff than we."

"Oh, no, you both had me beat hands down with planetary studies, and who turned out to be teachers? I remember you, Merc, driving your parents crazy, when you wanted holographic pictures of the universe, the galaxies and the planets all over your bedroom. And somehow, they managed to accommodate you. That was a gas."

"Yeah, I went to bed every night dreaming of the day that I would become an astronaut. And look who ended up taking 'the trip' of a lifetime."

"So what happened to those dreams, Merc? How come you let them slide?"

"I didn't. I just went in another direction. I became a teacher. Not to mention, life interfered."

"Oh, come on Merc, anybody can say that. Besides, it's never too late. I meant to ask you, 'Can you tell that I had a ball on this trip?'"

"Yep, we both can, just by looking at you. Your eyes are on fire and distant. And the worse part for us is listening and watching you and knowing that we were not right there at your side."

"Look at me, "guys". I want to make sure that your eyes are not turning green."

"Never mind our eyes. By the way, where the hell are our sandwiches? Every time you think about something else, you stop doin' your job. Now, we are really hungry. Times have not changed. We can't think on an empty stomach. You know that. Let's go. Let's eat."

Jupe jumped up and headed for the kitchen. Once he left the scene, Merc and Veni began checking out all the books and articles that were spread all over the place. It kept them busy, while Jupe did the "KP" duty. And as Jupe worked, his mind slipped back to an article he read in a February, Discover magazine. It discussed the fact that "the Catholic Church had put Galileo under house arrest for daring to say that the Earth orbits the sun." It went on to further explain that the church did not readily accept new scientific ideas. But in 1951, when the Pope accepted a brand new cosmological theory—the "Big Bang Theory," even the astrophysicists followed. That theory says, "The universe had a beginning, and that both time and space leaped out of nothingness." It seemed to confirm the first few biblical sentences in Genesis. This then, led to the acceptance of the notion that the entire observable universe—100 billion galaxies, each stuffed with 100 billion stars, stretching out more than 10 billion light-years, in all directions had credence.

"Are you two still there? You're very quiet."

"Yeah", "yeah."

"Do you remember Galileo?"

"Who, Veni or me? Neither one of us knew him personally, but I'm sure we both recall reading about him. Why?"

"I just read an old article about him and the Catholic church. It was very interesting. His works and images were reclaimed by the church in 1992; three hundred and fifty-years, after his death. There's nothing slow about them."

"Jupe, are you cooking in there, or what? And, why are you so suddenly interested in Galileo and the church?"

"Of course, I'm workin' and you will find out later about my interest in Galileo and the church."

"We do hope so."

"Do either of you remember what a light-year is?"

"No, but are we about to find out?"

"Yes. It's defined as a unit of distance equal to the distance that light travels in a vacuum in one year, 5,880,000,000 miles. I do prefer, however, the secondary definition: a very great distance, and amount of time, etc."

Veni just looked at Merc who hadn't finished shaking his head, when Jupe went on to explain, that the church also bought the idea that the cosmos burst into existence precisely 13.8 billion years ago and it has been expanding ever since. Today, even the "Big Bang Theory" is being challenged and it's only one-half century after acceptance. And, nobody has figured out why the cosmos is expanding at an accelerated rate. I know why it's expanding and why they can't figure it out. They can't figure it out because they had nothing to do with its creation. I'll share my non-scientific theory on the accelerated expansion with you later. If I forget, remind me. But somehow, I doubt that I will forget, because I still have to talk to you about Galileo and "The Hereafter."

"Well, I'm flabbergasted. How about you, Veni? Jupe, what's with you, and your sudden interest in the church and religion and the expanding cosmos? And by the way, will you please forget the religion and cosmos. 'Where the hell is the food?"

"Okay, everything is ready. Here ya go—enjoy, my friends. Pretty good, huh?"

"Whoa, Jupe we are so hungry, anything would taste good."

"I might be slow, but I'm not too bad a cook, even if I say so myself. So, what reaction do you think the Church would have if it heard about my journey?"

"What? You think we should know? "Veni, what do you know, that I don't know." Veni finally, out of curiosity, said, "Merc, how many times have you graced the halls of any church in the last five years? And Jupe, do you think that we are going to run off and tell someone about this? Not on your life. They will all think that we are crazy simply for having listened and encouraged you."

"Thanks, but what if I begin to prophesize, or develop new theories, because of this journey? After all, I did learn some very interesting things, and I know that they have affected my thinking about the world, the universe, galaxies, my Christian faith and life itself, both now and in "The Hereafter"—particularly, "The Hereafter." Just think, in Ancient times, I would have been burned at the stake, ended up in a mental institution, or an early grave. "Why did you have to ask me, where were you last night?" And by the way, how are the sandwiches?'"

"They are gone, but we are still hungry."

"That's too bad. This is not your local supermarket or restaurant, you know, 'how about some coffeecake?'"

"Do you have some coffee to go with it, my friend?"

"Geez, I'm sorry. I made a fresh pot, but forgot to serve it; *mea culpa*. I'll get it."

"Jupe, do you two know that it is almost two-thirty?"

"No. I was just thinking, it's wonderful what a thousand years can do. Isn't it? I can talk like this and have no fear of any reprisals, or condemnation. Wow, we have come a long way. I've been thinking about how Galileo went blind for his exploratory efforts and work with the Sun. And even today, we can't look directly at the Sun from earth, without damaging our eyes. And yet, I flew right by. I was so close. It was alive! And, here I am without any ill-effects sharing that moment. I can't tell you, how much I wish that I could do that again, and take both of you with me, of course."

"Jupe, Veni and I don't understand how you didn't turn into a cinder."

"You're right. I should be black dust right now. To be that close to the largest star in our Solar System, absorbing its magnificence, it was incredible. In case you have forgotten, I thought that I would remind you, that the Sun is just a little older than you, Merc, about five billion years. And, it's just a little larger than your waist, about 870,000 miles in diameter. Think about that.

"You know, you get funnier as this story goes on."

"I know, Merc. Now, picture this . . . I'm getting closer and closer to that giant red ball and all its fiery flares shooting away from its surface in all directions. I could see them quite clearly. The Prominences have huge jets of gas that extend into the atmosphere up to hundreds of thousands of miles high, and all I kept thinking was, no sense getting' my invisible 'arse' or anything else in whatever state I was in, singed. After all, it is too magnificent a journey not to be able to finish, come home and tell the story. Right?"

"Yeah, right."

"Do I detect some disbelief?"

"No, no, but eventually, we would really like to know, 'Where were you last night?'"

"What if I were to say, 'I visited the center of the Sun; its radiation zone—all 230,000 miles of its thickness. But for some reason, I wasn't made privy to its center core; its nuclear fission zone. Would you believe that?

"No, and by the way, can we get back to what ever happened to Neptune?"

"Oh, God, that planet was huge with a composition similar to Uranus—"ices," and rocks, hydrogen and helium. It's a gas giant, you know. It has several prominent features. There's a Great Dark Spot, which is as wide as the earth, and a Small Dark Spot and the Scooter. The Great and Small Dark Spots are huge storms that are swept around the planet by winds of about 1200 miles per hour. Would either of you like some more coffee or cake?"

In chorus, "No thanks."

"Back to Neptune . . . The Scooter was nothing to worry about, just a large area of cirrus clouds. Neptune also has four rings, it has 13 moons, not eight, as previously noted. I counted them. Triton, the largest Neptunian moon is the coldest object in the Solar System. It's—391° F and oddly, it orbits its mother planet in the opposite direction to the planet's rotation. Its gases give off a beautiful, iridescent, blue-green color. I know that you are not ready for this, because I wasn't. Neptune measures 30,777 miles in diameter. Remember Pluto? Its diameter is only 1,420 miles; a marble by comparison. Wow!"

A long pause ensued, while I flew through Saturn's ring. Somehow, I expected to be coated with some of the garbage and debris that perpetually floats in its orbit. As I was envisioning that, I realized that I never was touched by any of that stuff. Everything was moving so fast. The hole that I created as I flew through seemed never to have existed. After I left it, it closed itself almost as fast as it parted. If I had not popped through, I probably would have been caught in its gravitational pull and remained spinning there forever.

"Jupe, that's great, but we have decided, we have had enough for today, even though we can't wait to hear about "The Hereafter." Let's call it quits for now. Okay?"

"Sure, but how about tomorrow night? Do you want to come over? What are your schedules like?"

"Don't worry about our schedules. Simply tell us what time and believe me, we will be here. Are you sure that you are okay, Jupe?"

"Yes, I'm fine; just a little tired. And in case you don't know this. For the record, I do have to say, "*I Fell in Love with My Life When I Took This Journey.*"

They just smiled.

And "guys", do me a favor, read up on the planets, because I want you to double check my first-hand recollections. You might want to write them down. I know how you both love to write. Okay?"

"Okay, Jupe. We will see you tomorrow, right here at about 5:30 p.m., and we will not only bring some Chinese food, but our notes. Are you going to work tomorrow? Will you be sharing this journey with your co-workers?"

"Yes to work, and no to sharing. Now, I know that I don't have to tell you this, but I will to satisfy myself. Please keep what I'm telling you to yourselves. And please, Merc, don't tell Mary. I would greatly appreciate that. I may decide to write a book, or something."

"We wouldn't be surprised, Jupe. This story should be told, but we are your friends and we promise that we won't preempt your book, or tell a soul, not even Mary."

"Thanks. See you tomorrow."

As the door closed behind them, their heads were spinning. They had more than enough thoughts to keep them mentally preoccupied on their trip home. To say, nothing about the non-stop conversation about what they had just experienced and heard.

The next day dragged for all of them. They each had trouble waiting for the clock to strike five. They all were on fire.

All day, Veni and Merc struggled not only imagining, but trying to absorb exactly what Jupe had been telling them. The problem for them was amplified by the fact that they, being specially chosen science teachers to work with the astronauts at NASA daily, thought that they knew much more than any ordinary citizen. But what Jupe was saying, was so far removed from our country's baby-steps in space, they couldn't digest and evaluate all that material quickly enough. They could see it all, but the NASA programs were still simply involved with planetary and star picture taking fly-bys. Obviously, there is a great deal more to be learned.

And as they continued to mentally review Jupe's trip and compare it to our country's space odysseys, one thing became quite evident. Almost all of our missions were lacking a vital, crucial aspect . . . human involvement; human emotion even though Jupe said he did not have any emotion, his body revealed just the opposite as he spoke. Our United States Congressional members often argued about appropriations involving that very point in our space program, "Manned vs. Unmanned" space flights. Veni and Merc knew now having listened to and watched Jupe, that if you can't feel the emotion, your understanding about what you see beyond the scope of the lens is greatly diminished. No camera, no matter how powerful, can replace the sense of awe, the depth of vision in terms of a basic 360° panorama, and capture the true lens-eye colors transmitted to and etched on a human brain. How often have I said of a good camera picture, when sharing it with friends, "It really doesn't capture the true colors of that sunset. I guess you would have to have been there to really appreciate it."

Veni and Merc knew that their own emotions were running very high, just having heard the tale Jupe was sharing. This was more than just a story. It was history. He found it most difficult not to blurt out the whole story. He wanted to tell everyone. He did not count how many phone calls he and Veni shared throughout the day. But they had given their promise of silence to their friend and held true to it. Just the same, this whole thing was overwhelming and utterly unbelievable. Merc, throughout his day sat in total stillness. He tried to sense the great void, the vastness, the endless quiet, and all the unknowns that existed while flying by planets and in and around the stars. He was rendered speechless and motionless by his own thoughts.

After Merc left the office and the dinner order was complete, he ran to Jupe's place *tout de suite*. Veni was already there.

In the meantime, Jupe, all day was trying to control his feelings. He was having a very hard time with his nerves. He wanted to share everything with everybody, but he was afraid of what might be said, or worse still, done. So he did his best to keep his mouth shut. He succeeded. But many times throughout the day, as he retraced his fantastic voyage, his co-workers called to him and asked, "Hey, Jupe, are you okay? You look as though you're in a trance." He could feel the blood rush to his face. He was really embarrassed. On the dot of 5:00 p.m., he was but a figurative vapor. He was out the door. He was happy to get home, feed the fish, and change into comfortable clothes. He just wanted to relax a bit before Merc and Veni showed up.

He was setting the table when Veni rang the doorbell. Jupe opened the door.

Upon seeing Veni, felt as though he just wanted to wrap his arms around her and hug her for being such a good friend.

Veni bounced in saying, "Hi, Jupe, how are you tonight?"

"Jupe replied, "I'm fine." "Thanks for asking."

"Are you ready to fly again?"

"Oh, yes!" "Where is Merc?"

"He stopped to get our dinner. Remember?"

"No, I forgot. It has been a long day."

"Veni, I feel as though I have been flying all day. Can you answer the door? Thanks."

Jupe yelled, "Hey, Merc, what took you so long? We are starved. Wow! That Chinese food smells good. 'Let's eat.' And just like any little kid, he said, "What did you bring?"

Merc replied, "Oh, a little of this and a little of that, but you can bet it is definitely not as exotic as the universe."

As Jupe opened the cartons, he found shrimp in lobster sauce (his favorite), roast pork with mushrooms, chicken lo mein, egg foo young, egg-drop and wonton soup, Chinese vegetables, egg rolls, rice, tea and of course, some fortune cookies. He was ready to dive in. And so, they all did.

"With his mouth full, Jupe said, "Well, if you think that thi trip has been something fantastic up to now, just you wait unt you travel with me tonight. I was traveling at supersonic spee when we met last. Now, hang on, we're about to enter the spee of light. My gaseous eyes or their equivalent in my gaseous stat found it difficult to keep up with everything that was bounci around me. And, of course, I didn't want to miss a thing. went beyond belief. Trust me."

"Veni finally said, I would like to know more about yc feelings, Jupe. How did you feel? I know that you said that y were not cold, or hot; you were just there. But, you had to something. How about an emotion or two?

"Veni, I'm telling you. My mind was active. I could visualize absorb what was happening, but it didn't affect me as much would have in my own atmosphere and environment. The n I traveled, the more I wanted to move on, particularly wh

passed the giant, gaseous planets. Maybe that's where I could admit to a human twinge, a sense of emotion—a sense of fear. But, it felt very unnatural. It was as if my human feelings were displaced and vaulted. And yet, they were desperately fighting to be set free. Something was confining them. I felt as though something was at my side throughout this whole journey. I did not feel alone. There was definitely something there. I felt as though there were people all around. I could sense them, their spirits. But one spirit in particular was very strong. It was not real, yet super-supportive and extremely controlling; a super guide, a super spirit, a super 'something.'"

As Jupe looked up, he suddenly realized that Merc was looking at him very strangely. He never looked at me that way before. It was almost as if what he was seeing was frightening him, but I was too excited to question him. I should have just said, "Why are you looking at me that way? But, I didn't. I missed my opportunity and simply sank into my mind's abyss."

Once again, Jupe was staring at Merc, and not saying anything, and Merc was staring at him. From his expression, Merc could tell that Jupe was in some other world. What Merc did not know was that at that very moment Jupe was unable to speak, because he felt as though his skin was going through a metamorphosis, regressing perhaps into his journey's gaseous state. Merc not only felt uneasy, but he sensed that Veni had become quite frightened.

They both were sitting quiet, but appeared stunned and looked quite pale, as if they didn't know what to say, or do. Merc was the first to speak, and he did so in his usual controlled manner. "Jupe, Jupe, come back! Where are you?" He spoke gently, as if not wanting to disturb a sleeping child.

"Oh, I'm sorry. I was just feeling a little strange. I think that the strong emotions I should have felt during my travels are hitting

me now. I am getting more and more nervous and excited just thinking about and visualizing what I have been through. And too, I have been projecting myself into upcoming scenes. I tell you, if ever fear was in my bones and body, and traveling with me, I would have been jolted dead passing the three planetary gas giants; Uranus, Saturn, and Jupiter, the Seventh, Sixth and Fifth planets from the Sun, respectively. Their distance from the Sun, however, wasn't the problem. It was their size. I don't ever want to come face-to-face with anything that huge again. Not that I ever will. And I can't begin to fully explain, what I am about to say, even in retrospect. In human terms, it is utterly indefinable . . . indescribable . . . unfathomable. There is nothing on Earth to compare with the size of those three planets. Not even the Earth itself."

"Whoa, Jupe, what are you saying, that there is nothing on our planet that compares with them size wise? Is that what you are telling me?"

"Yes. You got it. Nobody ever thinks about that. But I will try to share with you one of the most memorable and awe inspiring moments of my odyssey. I thought that the planet Neptune was large, and it was. It is. In fact, it is the largest object that I had ever seen in my lifetime. Let's see, how am I going to put all of this into its proper perspective? Perhaps, this will help. The Earth is approximately 8,000 miles in diameter; Neptune is approximately 31,000 miles in diameter. Now, think about the Earth. Then imagine if you can, a sphere that is about four times larger in size, subtract 1,000 miles from its diameter and you'll have the picture. I know that I'm asking the impossible. And, yes, it does take a great deal of imagination. So, "guys", I ask you, 'How can I expect anyone to experience what I did, when those three orbs, Uranus, Saturn and Jupiter, came barreling at me, one after the other while they were growing in size, each in turn?' 'Are you really still with me? Have we finished all the food? Is there anything left?'"

"Veni said, I think so. Do you want me to check and heat it up for you?"

"No, no, I will take care of it. Hey, did you open your fortune cookies yet?"

"Yes. Mine said that I was going to be an astronaut."

"Get out! You're kiddin' me."

"Yeah, I am. But it did say that I would soon be a groom."

"No joke. You better not tell Mary, or you'll be altar-bound before you know it."

Merc was extremely patient. He waited for me to crumble one of my fortune cookies all over the table. He shook his head. I was toying with him. I didn't tell him what the "big cookie secret" was until he screamed at me.

"Jupe, we are waiting. You're not playin' fair. Come on, what does it say?"

"It's short and sweet. It simply says, 'I am going to be a star,' how about that?"

They all laughed, as Jupe popped up to drain whatever food was left in all the scattered containers. There were meager remains. Merc almost looked embarrassed that he had not purchased enough.

"Hey, Jupe, while you are up, will you get us something to drink, and if you have any left over coffeecake, bring it along. Okay?"

"Sure, but remember, it's at least two days old. 'Hey "guys," did you have any time overnight to look at the universe information that I asked you to check?'"

"Their synchronized response, "Yes, we did." Now we are seeing too much of each other. We are beginning to think alike. Ouch! You know there is a lot of truth in fortune cookies. I am really hooked on Mary. In fact, I am thinking about asking her to marry me and settling down. What do you think?"

"What do I think? Merc, 'Why are you asking me?' Only you can answer that question. Ask, Veni."

"I just did. Well, Veni, what do you think? Actually, the same as you do, Jupe. "Merc, only you can answer that question."

"You two are really a big help."

"Jupe, will you be my Best Man?"

"Of course, I'm honored that you asked me."

"Oh, good . . . I'll let you know, as soon as I ask Mary, and she hopefully accepts my proposal. I'll plan a very romantic evening for that big event of course, but first I want to ask her parents' permission."

"Okay, digressions, digressions, let's try to concentrate. Please don't become distracted. Thanks."

I passed Neptune without even a whimper. Then suddenly, I was face-to-face with Uranus. It's a 1,000 miles wider than Neptune."

"We know. We did our homework."

"Let me see your notes. Let's all go over them together. Okay? If I need to change anything, I will. The Universe is constantly changing. The planets are changing. There are hundreds of new discoveries. In fact, did you know that they have just received updated information from Hubble and other probes? I read that some of the info I just shared with you about Neptune has already changed. They even have identified the bright spot that I saw hovering beyond Pluto and I didn't mention it, because I thought that is was insignificant. How wrong can one be? They have already named it. It is called Sedna. It now is the farthest object from the Sun . . ." As of today, that is.

"We know, Jupe. We were going to share that latest tidbit with you tonight, as you traveled in the heavens. We will change what we have to as we go."

"Merc, you two have been taking notes all along."

"Yes, we have. We wanted to surprise you, but they are quite sketchy—just tidbits. So now that you know, maybe we can record the information going forward. 'What do you say?'"

"Good idea. But, I'm still living in the dark ages. The only recording device I have is a tape recorder and plenty of tape."

"Besides Jupe, Veni and I have decided, when you discuss "The Hereafter," we definitely want that input recorded for posterity—even if only on tape. It must last forever."

"Cute, Merc—I'm glad that I did not move too far beyond Neptune, because they have most recently noted some dramatic events on that planet. Those distinctive spots—The Great Dark and Small, and the Scooter have changed. Here are my notes. While I look for my recorder and tape, and set it up you and Veni can read about it. I saved it for you."

"You know, I'm still reeling from the size of URANUS. Oh, and its color. It is the most gorgeous blue-green that I have ever seen. It comes from its atmospheric methane. The cloud top temperature exceeds—350º F. It sits on a strangely tilted axis, which makes it roll on its side as it orbits the Sun. It has 11 rings of rocks interspersed with dust lanes. The rings contain some of the darkest matter in the Solar System. Did you know that? He never took a breath. He didn't give me a chance to answer. He just kept on going. And it has 15 known moons that are known to be icy and hang out beyond the rings. What a scary sight that was. Can you imagine the immensity of that globe and watching those moons move? Then add, all its other activities happening simultaneously, as it spins in space? I saw it, and I just know I trembled at the enormity of what I saw. What a self-defining experience!

Veni and Merc were awed by Jupe's changing expressions, his unabashed emotional release of his first-hand, hard core, sensitive, and out-of-this-world knowledge. Jupe was trembling as he spoke about what he had experienced. They wondered just how Jupe would manage to release his information about the next two planets, which were larger still. How would Jupe handle their presence in space . . . their presence in our universe?

Suddenly, without warning, Jupe yelled, "WOW! You better duck, I'm movin' on to bigger and better things. How is the recorder working?"

"It's fine. There's plenty of space . . . it's spinnin'. Keep going."

"You know SATURN'S expansiveness is actually a result of its rings which stretch outward from the planet's surface to about 260,000 miles. Can you picture that? Not only did I face a surface diameter of just under 75,000 miles, but a bunch of narrow ringlets in its main rings that are made up of icy particles—lumps and chunks that measure from tiny to large. Some are several yards across. And all of it is less than one mile thick." And I was in the middle of it.

As they looked at Jupe, they saw him fading at times, but they did not want to stop him. He was surely on a proverbial "roll." This was not only diarrhea of the mouth, but the mind. They just sat, smiled and nodded; hopefully encouraging. It was working, because Jupe just kept going.

Jupe announced, "And now, the *piece de résistance!* The largest of the large—*JUPITER!* I have no earthly words to define its size. Our records note a diameter of 88, 850 miles. Earth is just a little less than 8,000 miles in diameter. Right?"

"Veni said, "more, or less, Jupe."

"Are you sick of listening, "guys?" Are you bored to death yet? To me, it's exciting. It's incredible! Yes, I know. How many more times am I going to say that?"

"Not to worry, my friend. It is a tale worth telling and hearing. But, we think that you might be tiring. So, why don't you just read aloud our notes about Jupiter, and add or subtract what you want. Lend your own spin; how's that?"

"Great! That's perfect."

"Here are the notes. We kept them brief, and we have our own copies. So, we will read along and check our work."

They all sat quietly as Jupe read the following:

JUPITER:

It is the fifth planet from the Sun and the first of four gas giants. It is the largest and most massive of the planets with a diameter about 11 times that of the Earth, and has a combined 2.5 mass of the eight other planets. An outer mantle of hydrogen and helium merge into a gaseous atmosphere. Its rapid rate of rotation causes the clouds in its atmosphere to form belts and zones that encircle the planet parallel to the equator. The most prominent cloud feature is a storm called the Great Red Spot, which consists of a spiraling column of clouds three times wider than the Earth that rises about five miles above the upper cloud layer. Its diameter measures approximately 88,850 miles. Wow! Jupiter has one thin, faint, main ring, inside of which is a halo ring and tiny particles extending toward the planet. There are 16 known Jovian moons.

"Hey, I skipped Saturn and Uranus. No you didn't. Oh, good, I was just going to say they parroted pretty much what I just shared with you. Okay, so skip it. Now, I have a question for you. When you were writing your material, how did you feel? What were you thinking? Sorry, that's obviously two questions. But, I am pretty sure that you can handle it, right guys?

We agree, in order to have the same feelings as you, we would have had to journey to the outer reaches. Trying to imagine and visualize the size of Jupiter, for example, is unfathomable. How big is a sphere that measures 88,000 plus, miles in diameter? That's almost like asking us, 'How wide is wide?' We would have no reference for any object that size. In fact, we were so curious about it, that we called the Auto Club and asked them to give us the mileage between the Olympic National Park in the State of Washington on the West Coast to Van Buren, Maine on the East Coast. We thought that it might just give us a proper perspective. Amazingly, it's only 3,375 miles and if we were to drive, it would take 60 hours and 20 minutes. That's if we traveled the closest route in a straight line. That put your speed into perspective, but size is still hanging out there. No pun intended. We would have to multiple that U.S. mileage by 26.33 times to have it equal the diameter of Jupiter. Jupe, that's downright scary. In answer to your second question, we immediately thought about how infinitesimally small we are. We all are. What about you Jupe? Do you feel infinitesimally small at this point?"

"As I have said, 'I will never be the same.' If I had approached Uranus, then Saturn and then, Jupiter in that order, watching them each in turn stretch wider and wider across the black horizon, and if I had my full faculties and emotions in tacked, I would have died of fright. Without question and without hesitation, I would have become part of our Universal void."

"What we don't understand, Jupe, is the fact that we are involved in the space environment every day at work, together with the astronauts, engineers, scientists, astronomers, astrologers, and selected students and have quite often been in the company of many others who are involved daily in that work, and we don't think that any of us truly understand, or appreciate, the enormity of what we are trying to do. Perhaps that's because we all break the Universe into little bits and pieces. We all work on a chunk or two in each group, and we are so in awe of what we see that we can't imagine what we all would be like if we went with you on your fantastic voyage. You are right. Life would never be the same. It would take on a totally new, indefinable, perspective. I think, Merc said, that I might even give up my life to journey as you did. And, I don't think that I would be speaking out of turn to say that Veni and my co-workers would feel the same as I."

"You know, not to diminish in any way what our country is doing, or what our astronauts have already accomplished, but it is miniscule compared with the totality of just our one Universe."

"What are you saying, Jupe? That there are Universes beyond our Universe?"

"I don't know. But, I traveled quite a distance beyond Pluto and there seemed to be no end in sight. In fact, if I am not mistaken, we soon will be jolted into a new space perspective. And even though I really wanted to go home, something within was making me want to stay. I wished that I could have traveled farther. But being human, even without my body and emotions in tacked, I had a deep desire to come home, when I reached Pluto. I told you that. Once I passed Jupiter, I knew that the rest of the journey was going to be a 'piece of cake'. After that what would be left, Mars? And we have already landed our rovers and explored that planet. That was funny. I actually watched first-hand as our rovers did some of their work. How about that? Earth, we should know a little bit about that place; then, Venus, (Hi, Ho, Veni) which is similar to our home. After all, if I am not mistaken she is considered our "sister planet." Finally, hot as hell, Mercury. But, don't get overly excited and think that we are near finished. Wait until I tell you about the 'stars and the 'hereafter.' But if you don't mind, I'm going to quit for now. "Are you two up for another assignment?"

"Oh, no, what do you think this is school?

"Veni, is he complaining? Will you?"

"You'll like this one. I want you to tell me in a 1,000 words or less, what you expect to find in the 'hereafter.' That's not too bad. We've discussed it many times. So, I know that you will have a lot of fun with that one—right?"

"Jupe, my friend, you are crazy. But, we'd miss you if you weren't here. We'll take a shot at your assignment. However, we'll do that one together. It just might be some diversionary fun. Jupe, in case we didn't tell you, we will be going out of town for a few days on a special assignment. They just confirmed it today. We have both been selected to attend a special Budgetary Conference. Before we go, we'll slip our thoughts under your door. That way you will have something to compare to the real thing."

"Okay my friends. Where are you off to?"

"They are sending us down to Washington, D.C. for some important budget hearing . . . boring! It's a nice time of year though—Cherry Blossom Time. Before Veni starts home, she is going to visit a friend. And I am thinking of asking Mary to join me for a long weekend. It might be a perfect time to "pop the big question," while we are walking under the Cherry Trees. There's only one problem, I'm still trying to get my full itinerary out of my boss. Right now, we are scheduled to leave Wednesday evening and we are expected to finish on Friday afternoon. I'm hoping that Mary will meet me on Friday and we can both come back on Monday. That sounds like a great plan, doesn't it? Isn't it a wonderful idea?"

"Jupe piped up, you are right, that sounds great. In fact, I will try to meet you there."

Merc fell dead silent. Veni giggled.

Jupe simply laughed.

"Jupe, you are joking, of course. Aren't you?"

"Well, my fortune cookie did say that I was going to be a star. What better place to start than in the Capitol. You know my love of politics."

Merc's mouth dropped open and no words came out. Jupe finally let go and laughed heartily.

"Of course, I'm kidding, Merc. You see little enough of Mary, without someone horning in and having to share her. It sounds like a very romantic idea. You'll enjoy every moment together, I'm sure. And, when you pop the question and she says, 'Yes.' Then you'll both return on cloud nine. For now, I'm just jealous."

"Well, you do have *Gallactia*."

"Since you both will be going away, would you like to finish the planets tonight? We only have four to go."

"Yes, Jupe, let's do that. Then, when we return, you will have added your thoughts, corrections, suggestions, etc. to our writings. Come on, let's continue to read."

"Okay."

They then fell silent as they each picked up copies of Merc's and Veni's writings. They began where they had left off with the concluding statements about Jupiter.

"Hey, let's move on to Mars and the Earth. Okay?"

"Yep"

MARS:

It's known as the Red Planet, the outermost rocky planet—fourth from the Sun. But, you knew that. However, did you know that when the astronomers first observe canal-like markings on the surface and dark patches they were thought to be vegetation? They thought there was life on the planet. We later found out, when on site, that the canals were an optical illusion and the dark patches are areas where the red dust that covers most of the planet has blown away. Residual dust in the atmosphere gives the Martian sky a pinkish hue. I saw that, as well as, several large, extinct volcanoes, including Olympus Mons, which is 370 miles wide and 15 miles high . . . the largest known volcano in the Solar System. It is now known that there is water on Mars. Mars has two tiny, irregularly shaped moons, Phobos and Deimos, which are small in size indicating that they may be asteroids captured by the gravity of Mars. Diameter: 4,217 miles

THE EARTH:

It is the third of the nine planets that orbit the Sun. It is the largest and densest rocky planet and the only one known to support life. 70% of the Earth's surface is covered by water, which is not found in liquid form on the surface of any other planet so far. At the heart of the planet the solid inner core has a temperature of about 7250° F. The Earth has one natural satellite, the Moon, which is large enough for both bodies to be considered a double-planet system. Diameter: 7,926 miles

"Okay, Venus and Mercury will be our next stops."

VENUS:

It is a rocky planet, second from the Sun. It spins slowly backward as it orbits the Sun, causing its rotational period to be the longest in the Solar System—about 245 Earth days. It is just slightly smaller than Earth. Venus is the brightest object in the sky, after the Sun and the Moon, because its atmosphere reflects sunlight strongly. Venus is the hottest planet, 900° F with winds of 220 mph. It is covered with craters, mountains, and volcanoes. It's the least hospitable place for life in the Solar System, but the brightest "star" in the sky. Diameter: 7,521 miles

MERCURY:

It is nearest to the Sun. And, because it is the closest to the Sun, it moves faster than any other planet. I guess it tries to escape the heat. It travels at an average speed of 30 miles per second—completing an orbit in just under 88 days. I told you, you were fast Merc, and hot. It is very small and rocky. Most of its surface is cratered, caused by meteorites hits, but it also has smooth plains. The planet rotates very slowly taking 59 Earth days to complete one rotation. A Solar day (sunrise to sunrise on Mercury is about 176 Earth days—twice as long as the 88 day Mercurian year. Extreme surface temperatures 800° F—minus 270° F. Diameter: 3,051 miles

When Jupe finished, he looked over at Merc and Veni and said, there is so much more for me to add. Did you really want me to cut my journey and information down like this? There is so much more, and the recent exploratory findings have been mind boggling. I am not going to feel comfortable, if I leave any of that information out."

"No, Jupe! You do what you want. We really did this in a hurry, so we did expect you to make changes. Be our guest."

"Oh, by the way my friends, please do me a big favor, do the writings on "The Hereafter" before you leave for D.C. Then, just slip them under my door." It will keep my nerves in check until you return, and I can think about how best to cover what I saw and heard on the subject. I know that you are anxiously awaiting my thoughts. I hope that I do not disappoint you. It may be quite different from what you expect. I'm really tired now. I have to stop. Let's call it quits. Okay?"

"Of course, and as we leave, let us just say that you might be very surprised about what we write concerning our 'hereafter' thoughts. Have a good night."

"You too, and try to be serious."

Jupe couldn't wait to clean up the mess they all made, and to hop into bed. He really was tired. As he placed his head upon the pillow a broad smile crossed his lips. Knowing Merc's and Veni's sense of humor, he was well aware of what they might write about the Hereafter, and he couldn't wait to read it. He just hoped that it wouldn't be too wild. As he left that thought, he drifted into a deep, well-needed sleep.

Veni and Merc were really hyped and they didn't feel tired. So, they decided to start Jupe's project immediately. They both had some thoughts that they wanted to quickly get down on paper. Merc actually felt as though Jupe had opened up the floodgates of his heavenly thoughts. He remembered that in the past he had asked some of his closest and dearest friends to share their beliefs on the subject. He shared them with Veni.

He said, "One expects to be able to meet and greet those she loved and lost, and also have the power to look down upon her family, share their joys and sorrows. Two others, both female—a widow and a single person—expect to just fade into dust. Yet, they each said emphatically, "I still want to believe that life will go on even if it is in a different state with those you knew and loved." One of the few men who answered the question did so reluctantly. He seemed not to want to even think about it. And when he did respond, it was a light-hearted response. "I want to have baseball and a new car." "That's honest, but what might your family think about that response?" The instantaneous come back was, "I hope that they all know how I feel about them and where they fit in." To me, the answer was humorous and poignant. He knows, they know, how much he loves them and therefore, they would not deny him two joys from his earthly life.

Nevertheless, with coffee cup in hand, Merc and Veni sat down to scribble some notes. Before they knew it, the hours had passed and it was well into the next morning. Now their thoughts had been recorded, not only for Jupe, but posterity. Of course, they will never forgive their friend for this one. They decided however that they were quite pleased with themselves and although it was quite late, or early, depending upon how they looked at it, they began to read what they had written—their own thoughts. Admittedly, they loved the choice of title and opening line, but hated the fact that they ended up with more questions than answers.

They both felt good about themselves as they placed their completed "assignment" into an envelope for delivery to Jupe in the morning. They made final arrangements to slip it under Jupe's door, before they headed off to their D.C. Conference.

Jupe upon awakening ran to check for the envelope under the door. He was thrilled. He loved the title. It was called:

"THE RECEPTION"

Jupe, just so you know, we began by asking ourselves
a very simple question. Have you ever truly
wondered how you might find "The Hereafter?"

We are not referring to a road map of the shortest distance from our earthly bonds to the "Pearly Gates." We are talking about its hospitality. What might the surrounding conditions be? What might be the condition of those you want to meet up with upon your demise? Will they be happy? Will they be sad? Will they be nondescript? Will they be recognizable to us and us to them? It left us wondering. Will they actually be?

We wondered whether the known, or "clandestine," meetings will be instantaneous, or many light-years away. Will we travel through a tunnel and visit times past as we go? Will they be good, bad, or a combination of both? Or, will we just find ourselves in a cavernous room with billions of others?

How about age? What might be the age of the persons you wish to embrace? Will they be at the age of their demise, and in that age's physical condition? Will they appear at an age that you want them to be at? Will they be at an age that some "Superior Being" has dictated? Will they be at an age in which they were most fruitful and productive? Will they have been freed from whatever illness, or catastrophic event, might have caused their death? Will they be at an age most recognizable to us? Or, will all the inhabitants be at the same age? Will we be able to find those whom we are looking for? We wonder.

Let's take a closer look at all of this. What if the loved-one passed away as a child, or when you were a child? How would you know them now, if they have been aging all this time? Will they have been aging? In that instance, neither might be able to recognize the other. Eh, what? Do you think that upon your death, you will be at the age most recognizable to all who knew you, when they knew you? Perhaps we will be able to pick the age we liked best. But, would that mean that we would only be able to be with those we knew at that age? We wonder.

Will all members of each family be together? What about friends? Where will they fit in this equation? Think about this . . . you are born into "Family A," but "Family A" is actually "Families A and B," and in some cases, due to second and third, etc. unions, this might be expanded. Now, you have neighbors in each place where you lived, where will they come in? You go to school and meet more people, students, and teachers, those who take you to and from. My, my, the "family" is growing. Not only do you go to grammar school, but high school and college and seminars, etc. And all along the way you bond with those you meet and greet. We shouldn't forget work. Think about all the jobs you held, and how many, many people you met. And, out of all those associations, you developed friendships. You met people you liked and some whom you didn't. Our "family unit" is getting crowded. Isn't it? How about falling in love, getting married, and raising your own children? They grow up and spread their wings (or shouldn't we use that terminology given our topic) and more and more and more and more people enter your life. We can't stop here, can we? How about our doctors and dentists and grocers, and mailpersons and retailers? Where will all those with whom we wish to reunite be located, given the humanity who has gained access to "heavenly homes" over the millennia? Oh, my . . . We wonder.

Will they all be clothed? Or, will they simple be dressed in "hereafter garb" . . . all the same. What will the temperature be? Will it automatically adjust to each deceased person's comfort? How about light? Will it always be daylight? Will there be a need for sunglasses, and sunscreen? Many, including me, think the new houses of today are too large. Let me tell you that mansion in the sky must be indescribable. How many rooms do you think it has?

How will we communicate? As we did in mortal life, or will there be a "hereafter language?" And then, if that be the case, how will we know it? How will we learn it?

Can you imagine the music that will play? Think about all those wonderful entertainers who have gone on before us. Will there be a giant juke box for us to select our favorite type of music? Or will we just have to think about the musician and a song, and it will play just for us in our new state of existence? Will all the actresses and actors be performing in their favorite roles? Or, will they be performing in new creations brought to life by all the other appropriate artisans who have settled in and are comfortable in their surroundings—whether new or old, but now, ever ageless. Will we be able to converse with all the people of note, who we admired, but could never reach? Would we want to? How about this, could we perform with them, if we felt like it? Would our talents be embellished, because we asked for that blessing? We wonder.

How about rich and poor? What type of money would we be using, if any? Would we have to purchase things to satisfy our needs, or would they just be provided simply by thinking about what we desire? How earthly our minds. Just can't seem to think in terms of "ethereal." And there is more . . .

Will we be greeted by the well-known, Saint Peter? Perhaps our lives were such that we will be greeted by a delegate, a representative of lesser renown . . . a substitute! Then we will know that we are in trouble. Won't we?

Right now, let me ask you, "Can you actually remember all your good deeds and nastiness throughout your lifetime?" Where do you fit between "goody-two-shoes" and "bi**h/bas***d" of the decades?" Could there be an "ethereal sin-machine—a huge slot machine with each of our names upon it?" The only difference between that one and a gambler's delight is that no coins are needed to operate it. Our earthly thoughts and actions provide the stimulus. In other words, how much good and bad did we generate throughout our human cognitive years? We wonder.

Wow! How about transportation? Will we arrive via a gigantic staircase, via a ride through a tunnel on turbulent clouds, or by some other vehicle not known to us, to reach our final destination? We decided that we would much prefer riding on soft billowy clouds. Will we be so happy to be free of our earthly cares, diseases and pain that we will fly as birds on the winds in timeless space? How about just vaporizing and being able to float in all directions, near and far, just by thought? Of course, that could be dangerous, if we are all floating and bumping into each other. Come to think of it, isn't this some kind of a trip?

And we haven't even addressed emotions and crowd control. Or is that too human? Can you imagine how crowded the Hereafter is? Think about how many species have already joined that world that's "out of this world." And think about this. If we cannot get along on our tiny planet with so many fewer inhabitants, what might we all do in that world? We shudder to think. We are beginning to think, given that thought, that it might to better just to let our bones and spirits stay on earth with all its problems. That doesn't make us very adventurous, does it? Not to mention the fact that this is a short, temporary journey. Time is so precious, and so fleeting. And for some, it is even more fleeting than others. We just realized something.

How about food and drink? Will we need it? Personally, we would prefer to just be self-fed. That would be possible in that environment, we are sure. Besides who will do the dishes? Maybe we will just eat air or clouds? If clouds, will the white billowy ones be like cotton candy and all the others more substantive? Will we drink or eat rain and snow and be satisfied? Perhaps there will be a heavenly hamburger stand. Better still, maybe we will be able to imagine any meal we want and it will appear, cooked to perfection and ready to eat. Will there be a local pub or two, or a hamburger joint, a short-order place?

This is a very interesting place that we are going to, isn't it? See how these little minds of ours keep thinking in terms of our present existence. But that doesn't mean that we can't state how we feel. Does it? We wonder.

We wonder too, if all the heavenly families will have to supply soldiers to fight a continuous war against Satan's angel armies, or if there will just be an eternal impenetrable wall of security. To keep peace in the Hereafter, particularly if we have mapped territories, we will all have to be "euphoricanized."

We forgot something very important. How about ethnicity? Will whites be white, and blacks be black and yellow races, yellow? Will we all carry the traits of our ancestry? Will we be the same height? Or will our new existence dictate that? Perhaps we will all be changed to reflect the opposite of what we were—the short will be tall and the tall, short. The obese will be skinny and the skinny, obese. Those with curly hair will have straight hair, and those with straight hair, curly. Will our eyes remain the same? Now, we are getting close to the point of "unrecognizable." Do you like that word? That thought?

Just think if this is all handled right, there will be no need for traffic lights or traffic police; we'll simply walk through each other. Wow!

Scientists have recently been baffled by the current rapid expansion of the universe. Could it be that the Hereafter mansion of many rooms is in the process of being expanded to accommodate the many new generations of residents? Will we be able to find our beloved pets? How about the pets of our youth? Gee, we wonder.

Could this be why so many have a fear of death, a fear of the unknown, as we know it? It might just be a wonderful experience. After all, most religions provide for a Hereafter of comfort. We wonder.

So, Jupe, is life in the Hereafter a reflection of life as we live it; simply a personal perception?

O, one more thing. We forgot. Will we be privy to all the historical unsolved mysteries? For example, "Who killed John F. Kennedy, and where is Hoffa? We would love to be filled in on these holes in history. I guess only time will tell. We will just have to wait and see.

We will end with this. We can only think in limited human terms. That's why we always come up with more questions than answers. And we find for us, that the answers to too many questions can only be found within—within the innate spirit that was planted at our beginning.

That's it. We hope you enjoyed our efforts, Jupe. See you soon.

When Jupe shared this with me, we both found it to be very funny.

Whoa! Perfect timing, the staircase has stopped again.

So, let me return to my story and my friend, Jupe. He was so glad to have Veni's and Merc's writing, because he was having such a hard time trying to control his nerves and jumpiness while his friends journeyed to Washington, D.C. for their Conference.

Jupe was very excited about Merc asking Mary to marry him and he couldn't wait to hear from Veni and Merc about their trip. They did spend part of the time together at the Conference, but Veni had her plans, while Mary joined Merc for the weekend. How nice. When the doorbell rang, Jupe jumped up to answer in a hurry. It was Veni. Obviously, she was first to arrive. She hadn't heard from Mary or Merc, so she was as curious as Jupe to hear about their weekend. They both started to talk about what Jupe has shared prior to the hiatus, but Jupe said, "Let's wait for Merc." Veni agreed.

She was extremely hyped about Jupe's next segment of his adventure—what he actually learned about the Hereafter. Merc finally showed up. It seemed like forever. Veni and Jupe did not have to ask him about the weekend and Mary's answer. He was beaming. The answer was written all over his face. Wow! How wonderful!

Jupe offered them a cup of coffee, and some fresh coffee cake. Then he began the most serious conversation of all. Veni and Merc were dead silent, and Jupe was more serious than he had been before they left. No one could believe what was happening, particularly Jupe. He was looking paler than before, and they both inquired as to whether or not he had been sleeping and eating. He said, "Oh, yes, to both questions."

Merc and Veni chatted about their trip, but both were anxious to hear from Jupe. So, after they settle down and got comfortable, Jupe once again picked up on his fantastic odyssey.

Okay, I am going to share with you the most startling of all things about the journey. This is most sacred and without equal. I guess the best way for me to begin would be by asking a question. "Does Heaven exist?"

Veni and Merc were dumbfounded, and neither said a word. They just let Jupe talk. He went on to say, "I believe I was in Heaven." It was the point at which I felt inner emotions. Even though I earlier said that I had none. Well, I sure did during this exploration of the space around me. The Heaven we filled with all the spirits of all those who had ever lived, and I was privy to their presence. I saw all the artisans since the beginning of time. In some cases, I was able to see them working on their latest masterpieces—their works of art. Musicians were preparing to perform their newest creations. I felt the heartbeats of all the military men and women who fought earth's many wars. I saw them all in their uniforms. I felt their emotions, their fears, and their devastation and willingness to accept all the inevitable that they were asked to face. I saw children playing and heard them laugh. I saw animals with their masters and frolicking with children. I saw the love in their eyes, spirits all. Their spirits were alive and well—surviving. No one was dead. No, everyone was alive, happy and healthy. And these scenes went on, and on, and on . . . they were endless. They were everlasting, eternal as the word itself. And, I saw and came to know God's mansion in the sky . . . His "house of many rooms." It went on ad infinitum. There were "rooms" for all who ever walked the face of the earth, and far more "rooms" than needed for future inhabitants, who too will live, thrive and be. The spiritual life that I saw and felt was beautiful. I wanted then to stay.

I felt the present of my mother, my father, my siblings, my family, my friends, and although dead, they were alive. Spirits joined and mingling every day in the Tomorrowland. It was not only exhilarating, but frightening. How will we be transformed and placed into such a beautiful survival? All I could think was, "Who will lead me, when it is my turn to join those of yesteryear, and those of today and tomorrow?" Jupe began to cry. He was so overtaken, but what he said was not the end. He had only just begun to share this story. He finally stopped long enough to say, "I'm sorry; I didn't mean to become so emotional, and overwhelmed again. Forgive me."

Veni and Merc quietly said, "Time to take a break."

Jupe seemed very tired, but he really wanted to go on. He was so anxious to finish his story. It meant so much to him. Veni and Merc insisted he rest. Although he didn't know it, he was fading again. He really was wondering exactly how to tell them the impossible. He actually now knew the answer that had plagued and puzzled humanity over the millennia, the history of man and his search for the answer to the question, "Where do we go when we die? The answer was now his, and he was afraid to share it. He was questioning himself. Will they believe me? Will they think I am crazy? Had the trip affected my mind? And beyond Veni and Merc who will believe what I am saying should I decide to tell the world? Who but God could create such a beautiful afterlife—a Hereafter so lovely, so believable?

While Jupe was thinking and resting, Veni decided to make a pot of coffee. It would not only help her and Merc, but bring Jupe back to life. They didn't want to force him to continue, but they were becoming somewhat anxious themselves. What could Jupe have possibly learned that was so fantastic? A little coffee—a little talk and Jupe was ready to roll on again. Jupe said, "This is what you have been waiting for, and all you ever need know."

I will tie the answer to the question, "Where do we go when we die?" to Jesus' words about our "forever" resting place in His Father's House/Mansion" of many rooms ***(Luke 14:2)***." Human thought and its literal creation of a "House/Mansion" of many "rooms" limits our understanding of "life-after-death" in our "Heavenly Home"—"The Hereafter," which has always been defined by those who were steeped in total repetition of the teachings shared down through the ages. And over all that time, everyone accepted what was passed on, even though it always left unanswered questions. How many, over the course of history, wondered and pondered, and then created their own answers to satisfy their needs? The biggest question was and still is, "How could there be "rooms" enough for all humans who have passed on and moved into the Hereafter?" That is impossible!

Suddenly, Jupe looked at Veni and Merc who were stunned, as they waited for the final point of the conversation on the Hereafter. He jumped up and said, "Whoa, it is dark and warm in here. Let's open a window. Okay?" Veni and Merc didn't say a word. They were watching Jupe, who was shrinking and beginning to glow. "I'm surrounded by spirits and stars. Can you see them?" Then without warning, Jupe said, "Goodbye," and flew out the window to join the stars of night. They never saw their friend again. He was on his way back to the Heavens.

Obviously, an extensive investigation began.

Merc and Veni were so distressed by what had happened that they did not realize he had not unlocked the "life-after-death" mystery for them. Well, he did for me, earlier. But before he left, he asked me to share his knowledge, if he wasn't able to. And if you will be patient and I am given more time, I will divulge the secret to all who will listen. Before I do so however, I would like to share my thoughts first. The ones I wanted to share with Jupe, Veni, Merc and ultimately God. Now that I have joined my friends, I am sure they will easily hear my conversation about these changes, as I share them with all of you. I hope my thoughts will become part of future generations and their tomorrow.

However, to enjoy these thoughts, you must bring a great sense of humor and a wide-opened mind to this presentation. I wrote my thoughts for Jupe around the same time Veni and Merc wrote their thoughts about the Hereafter for him.

Oh, my, the staircase is slowing down again.

I really must quickly share my remaining thoughts. They are not verbatim, but close enough. I entitled them ***"Absurd, More Absurd, Most Absurd and Beyond Absurd."*** And since they are from memory, I will leave the choice of which thought belongs to which idea to my reader's discretion. I hope you enjoy them, as much as I did creating them. And most importantly, I hope too, that you find them to be nothing less than interesting.

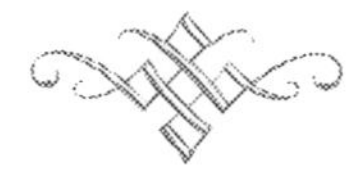

"Absurd, More Absurd, Most Absurd, And Beyond Absurd"

I hope that Jupe, Merc and Veni can hear this. They will surely declare me loony. But of course, I could say the same about Merc and Veni. I found their interpretation of the Hereafter, which they called "The Reception," very interesting. It's their personal thoughts about what they anticipated the Hereafter to be. It was quite funny. Jupe shared it with me, as you know, and I enjoyed it immensely. Some of their thoughts even mirrored my own, as originally written in my *"Absurd, More Absurd, Most Absurd and Beyond Absurd,"* which is what I am now going to share with you.

I wonder what everyone will think about my first questions, those I ultimately shared with Jupe, Merc and Veni, but never did. But now, it's for all those within earshot. The questions are, "Are humans God's monumental mistake? Or, are they merely a supernatural experiment? Is God testing His powers of creation through us?"

If I am given the opportunity, I will ask God, ***"Do you consider the creation of humans to be a monumental mistake?"*** For now however, I think it best to leave that thought with all of you and move on.

Some of my thoughts have pressed on me for years, and for many reasons. We were created to be responsible for the earth and all that's in it and on it. Being of superior knowledge, why are we knowingly destroying our own environment? Surely, we can find the means to live amicably in peace. However we are so aggressive, declaring wars, or even killing one individual. Why do we not recognize and accept other's points of view? Each recognizing the others right to live freely, as they choose. If we did, there would be no need for capital punishment, firing squads, lethal injections, electric chairs, gas chambers, etc. All these things would become obsolete, noted, and relegated to museums.

Then too, we create so many "natural disasters." And while we are creating them for ourselves, we create them for all of God's creatures' great and small. You know, the things affecting those totally unable to defend themselves against our thoughtless destructive behavior. We, the very ones placed here with a higher level of intelligence, to protect and care for those unable to protect themselves against the ravages of our thoughtlessness. So who really deserves God's angel wings?

Consider all the animals that have died, since the beginning of time, due to chemical spills, road rage, fires, floods, scientific experimentation, and inhumane treatment of all kinds. And, all because they were unfortunate enough to be born among us, chattering, singing, purring and doing what they were born to do, and do best. Now think of all of them protected behind the Pearly Gates in the Hereafter. Will there be room left for any of us in eternity? It will be mighty crowded. Maybe we should consider dying now in order to preserve a spot for ourselves. At the very least, perhaps we should make a reservation.

Given all of this, I repeat, could humanity be God's biggest mistake? We certainly are far from perfect. We would be the first to admit that to our Creator, wouldn't we? We are no match for our Creator. We will never reach that level of intelligence, cleverness, or creativity. Think about that. Can we substantiate anything with regard to human creation? Did we perhaps create ourselves? Did our parents breathe life into themselves? When was the last time humanity created anything earthly? How about a leaf, a tree, a rose, an animal, or a star for the Heavens?

Have you ever thought about, or asked yourself, "Is there a planet, unknown to us, hiding human and animal forms that mirror our own in fossil form just waiting to be discovered?" And, if those remains were unearthed in our lifetime, it would emphasize and define another theory of mine, that we may very well be our Creator's continued and on-going experiment. Now, that's interesting. Maybe we are just the beginning, a small part of a refinement process that will take millennia to polish, cultivate and ultimately lead to a more perfect humanity. Just think if this were to happen, how many years of investigations, speculations and suppositions would follow. Would our search for "Aliens" intensify, or diminish?

Who is to say that we are not the "Aliens" of the universe(s)? Survivors of the planets we seek to join and study. Perhaps our innate desire to travel into space is actually a calling home from our original lands of birth, our Own Grand Adventures, to seek and retrieve a particle of our past. Are we looking for ourselves?

I have said on many occasions that I would like to have an opportunity to speak with my Creator to discuss some parts of his creation. I would respectfully like to offer a few suggestions to improve upon the human body. And in turn, those changes would lead to improvements in other parts of our life. But, one of my major questions to God would be, "If you had to do it over again, would you change your mind? Would there be any specific changes that you would like to make? I would like the mind and the Will to be channeled to loftier pursuits. To formalize and crystallize the possibilities of a glorious society built on respect, elegance, calmness, quiet, love and peace. Frightening thought, isn't it?

Regarding our Will and our mind, I know what I would like to see in the future. But remember, it is based upon the past and the present, and my limited human intelligence and knowledge. I would start with the mind, and the use of Will. I definitely would keep our Will in place by refining it to control our aggressions, our inability to live neighborly lives with all our planet's inhabitants. Make sure that all the Wills of all people were in sync. How many problems would that resolve? All arbitrations and negotiations, if necessary, would be analyzed and amicably transformed, changed to everyone's satisfaction.

This would insure that all dictators, oppressors and self-serving individuals would be denied the ways and means of doing what they do best, dominate. This could possibly mean no more war. All manmade weapons of destruction, including armaments, explosives, chemicals, future technological discoveries, etc. would be destroyed and nevermore created, developed, produced, sold and/or used. There would be no more Will, desire or creative thought to invent them. We could channel these thoughts and accompanying talents to provide for all peoples needs to live sanitary and healthy lives. Eliminate torture to secure information for ulterior motives and personal negative purposes. However, I am not presuming to tell God what to do, just carrying on a simple conversation. I'm sure that I will be judged fairly. I simply want to share my thoughts as any child would with his father. Perhaps He will laugh. I hope so. And, I hope you do too. Trust me, my God can and does laugh. Of course without question, that will always depend upon the joke.

Now, for the ultimate, some beyond absurd:

I would like physicians to be able to diagnose without the aid of CAT scans, PET scans, X-Rays, etc. And be knowledgeable enough, not only to cure with all natural medications and the touch of their hands, but have the ability to perform all intricate surgeries with futuristic rays—no pain, bloodless and accurate.

And in keeping with this, I would also like *Human/Pets Parts Stores* on earth. I can envision them. Humans would simply walk into these establishments and purchase whatever they or their pets might need, whether it is to replace parts destroyed by illness, catastrophe, accident, or desire, even something to make humans happier. Some of these items are already available, but unaffordable and in short supply. I foresee some exclusions in the beginning, for example, new heads and brains. Strict restrictions would apply in order to avoid the unwanted. Purchases must be for self, or pet owners and replacements must be made under control. How about genes? Oh, to be able to buy some genes. That would be interesting. Wouldn't it? We would however need qualified persons to handle these implants and changes.

Now, without a problem, I can envision several changes to the human body that would improve our lives. For example, could we consider in-body plumbing? No, no, no, better still, make all eliminating functions, internal rather than the external processes we presently have? Just think of all the benefits internal functions rather than external functions would provide:

- Save time
- Save money (no need for toilets, toilet paper, plumbing, cleansers, air fresheners, built in fans). Wow!
- We would never be caught short again
- We would never have to queue-up
- There would be no need for toilet seat covers
- It would be so much cleaner and certainly more controlled

One might even say, "What a relief." But, being who and what we are, I am sure we would survive, and come up with some funny new material, new commentaries regarding the changes in our "end process." And by removing the endless process of eating and eliminating we resolve the need to expel gas. There would be no need for embarrassing social flatulence. We would no longer have to fart around with the current vulgar term "fart." Strike it from the dictionary. Sorry Webster. I am not recommending giving up eating. Why eliminate joyful events? Simply change the process of elimination. "Hallelujah!"

However we might want to alternate eating. That would really help the above mentioned process. I know, this is not only ABSURD, but very strange. However, I do love the thought. Do away with all food? Never. How could I even suggest that? Let's just say, whenever we become hungry, we would simply think about what we want and it would be made ready for us. Perfectly cooked and seasoned. No need to chew or swallow. Make it strictly a mental phenomenon. That's how I envision meals in the Hereafter. We would still smell and taste the food. Who would want to lose that capability? Let's not lose something that provides perfect satisfaction.

- ❖ No more hunger, lunch breaks or starvation
- ❖ Save lots of time and effort
- ❖ Save money
- ❖ Save lives—animals, birds, fish, humans, etc.
- ❖ No more pots, pans, stoves, ovens, microwaves, etc.

Now that I have taken care of the *internal* body, I would like to discuss changes to the *external* body. This is one of my favorites, one of the best. I would like to eliminate daily washing. To me, that would be great. Have the body, our skin, simply refresh itself overnight. We would awaken with new skin and ready to go. There would be no need for bathing, and we would feel as though we had. There would be no need to "freshen up." We would remain fresh all the time. The benefits:

- ❖ No need for towels, face clothes, bath mats
- ❖ We wouldn't have to wait to use the tubs, showers, etc.
- ❖ There would be more room in the washing machine
- ❖ There would be no need for body lotions, creams, etc.

This is one for the more mature folks. How about wrinkle-proof skin, and firm, well-toned muscles, no matter what the age? Somehow that sounds good to me.

Would you like to eliminate perspiration? That would be wonderful too. No more need for anti-perspirants, deodorants, colognes, and perfumes. Our bodies would always be pure, clean and fresh. There are obvious benefits:

- ❖ Save money
- ❖ Eliminate allergies
- ❖ No offensive odors

Let's discuss the physical attributes of *the head* and *the face*. How about no sinus infections, eye strain, blemishes, poor skin. Ah, yes, everyone's skin would be perfect, no matter what the color. It would be wonderful not to have to wear glasses, and have the eyes automatically adjust to the sun, and focusing. And, wouldn't it be fantastic to wake up in the morning and have your eyes change to the color of your choice? Now, that would be exciting.

Teeth, I must address teeth. What a pain! No more cavities, or replacements, please. They should remain permanent. They should grow as we grow. No first and second sets. No, no. They just grow, larger as we grow larger, until they arrive at perfection. There should be constant pleasant breath. How about that? And of course, they should be perfect "pearlies" for each mouth. There are probably too many benefits to innumerate for this one . . .

- Best smiles all over the world
- Save money, lots of money
- No more pain, lots of comfort
- My apologies to all dentist, orthodontists, oral surgeons, implant specialists
- Save time, no more lengthy appointments
- No more numbing shots
- No more drooling
- No need for tooth brushes, tooth pastes, mouth wash, dental floss, picks, etc.
- Food, if we decide to continue to eat as we do now, would finally know its place among the permanent "pearlies"

And men, could you live without beards? No more shaving. If I were to guess, I would say, you would say, "Yes." Unless of course, you want to grow a beard to change your appearance, that could be optional.

I would like no more ear problems. Eliminate wax, and buzzing, and ringing, and the causes of Vertigo, not to mention deafness.

Let us not forget our "stringlets" and "curly locks." Our hair! My, my, my, would you like to control your hair by just thinking about it? What style and thickness would you prefer? Old hair could be vaporized, simply disappear. Never to be seen again. And of course, we would have to control the color. That's really no problem. Just think about it and voilà; it would happen. Oh, the options are endless and grand. And the weather would have no effect at any time. Men, this recommendation would also include you. How about the benefits?

- No need for "perms" (Now, there's a blessing)
- No need for bleaching and dying
- No need for Beauty Parlors or Barber Shops (Sorry)

How about perfect fingernails and toenails—no chipping, or cracking, or splitting or growing beyond the most beautiful shape and size? Can you imagine? They would grow into their proper state for each stage of our lives. They would come with special characteristics too. For ladies, fingernails would change color to match and blend into the color of their clothing. Love it!

The last would be the most difficult. No more disease. This could, if not controlled lead to over-crowding. We would have to have a built-in dying system, a dying off process. Not like the one we have now. We would know, as we do now, from the start that we cannot live forever on the planet and in the state we are in. We would have the choice of expiration. It would be with you, God, a collaborative decision. One dictated by need, the need to perhaps move on to our "Next Assignment." The choice of death would be but one. Go to sleep and gently move on. Since God knows where we all will go, it will be easy for Him to find us. That thought is so beautiful. Maybe we could think about an unusual removal from *earth*. Something simple, like flying into the sky like Jupe, and joining those already settled in the Heavens. Benefits:

- Save money
- No need for us, or others to choose all the burial accoutrements
- No need for those who didn't keep in touch to view your body and tell you how good you look
- Or, that the right outfit had been chosen for you
- Or, that you look good in pink, or blue
- No need for burial plots and headstones
- If you are the last to go, who will visit?

It is better to be kept in another's heart and memory than in a box, or urn in the ground or Mausoleum. Don't you think?

Outlaw all foul odors. I could name quite a few. In fact, more than a few, but I will let you choose your own. Now, there is a little fun for you.

I will end on a positive note with a wish for all whom I left behind. No need to plant, transplant and buy garden beauty. For each tree and flower that dies on earth, new saplings and seedlings will grow, just as I believe they now do in the Heavens above. May those on e*arth* always enjoy it in a pristine form with fragrant soil, trees, flowers, and refined air. Glorious! Heavenly!

"Hey, I'm still moving.

That is good, because I have a lot more to share. I must define for you what I mean by "Our Next Assignment," where and what "our room" is in God's mansion in the Hereafter, and our Life Everlasting, Shoreless Sequels."

"Everlasting Life, Shoreless Sequels"

EVERLASTING LIFE
WHAT IS IT?

It is whatever you want it to be,
whatever your heart tells you.

It can be mystical. It can be inspiring and lead to a sense of spiritual mystery and awe. It can be an innate part of your being, planted at birth. It is what you believe it to be.

I believe it is a warehouse of all souls who have ever lived with each one readying for their Next Assignment, their Next Grand Adventure.

WHERE IS IT?

Wherever you want it to be!

For some it is just a figment, a fairy tale, a place to go after life has ended. An everlasting place of rest earned for having lived an exemplary life. Yes, it can be mythical to those who have no faith or belief. Or, it can be non-existent.

Most recognize Everlasting Life as a part of Heaven. But then, where is Heaven? The majority of those who have a strong faith and belief in its existence point up to the sky, when discussing life after death and everlasting life.

I have never heard anyone in my lifetime mention the center of the earth with its extreme heat and molten lava as representing Heaven. Perhaps that area is reserved for Satan and Hell.

During a lifetime, Heaven can be in the heart, or in the mind, particularly as one grows older and gets closer to its shores. It can be when we begin in earnest to understand our frailty and lack of knowledge, and when we walk through the Veil of the Heavenly Mist to join all past souls. And even though we have been there before, it can be upon returning to the "Pearly Gates," that we still call out in wonder and fear, "Hello, is anyone here?"

At that point, the most burning questions have to be, "Oh, God, will the expectations of my faith again rise to this occasion?" "Did I meet your expectations living this latest Assignment?" "Will You, God, greet me as expected with opened-arms and love?" "Will you once again bless my *Everlasting Life*, my *Next Assignment*, and my *Next Grand Adventure*?"

Having said this, I will now answer the question that I posed throughout this book. "Where do we go when we die?" Jupe assured me that we all will be going back from whence we came, to our room in God's mansion in the sky—our permanent Hereafter homes in the endless galaxies of earth. ***SPACE IS GOD'S MANSION; AND THE STARS ARE ITS MANY ROOMS. Always have been, always will be. AND THOSE STARS ARE THE SPIRITS OF ALL WHO HAVE EVER LIVED AND DIED.*** They are filled with love, and that love makes them shine and twinkle every night. They live in the land of their eternity. That land of believers. And upon death, we all return to *"Our room, Our Star."* The very star we came from when we were born.

Those who left the earth without love, or feeling unloved, will find it on their way home. It takes time I'm sure, to transition from earthly to Heavenly space. But it gives each spirit time to review, regroup and find everlasting peace. You know the peace that transcends human understanding. We come from love and we return to love. After all, where does love come from but on high? Nothing more needs to be said.

Oh, my, lucky me, the Heavenly mechanics are keeping my staircase moving. So, I will continue to share my thoughts, while I still have time to do so.

The joy of death is in the giving up of life, as it slips away, while we are returning home from our latest journey lived in love. But obviously, the best part can be found in the fact that we did not die. We live on in Eternity, and continue to live in spirit in the hearts of all those who cared for us and loved us. Albeit perhaps too few. In death there is eternal and earthly life. But to live on we must accept without question the promise in death. Everlasting means just that, Everlasting.

My goodbye is only a goodbye for those who fail to believe in my "afterlife" life. My goodbye is only temporary. We will meet again. I will remain alive in spirit, today, as yesterday, tomorrow and always. ***For I do have a room in God's expansive world in the sky; I've always had it, even before I was born to live this last Assignment. God's world is not a structure with walls, windows, doors and rooms. No. It is the whole of Heaven, all that exists beyond earth.*** **Now you know where I believe we will be going when we die.**

For those who find this incredible, or fail to find any comfort in this thought, I then must insist that you find your answer to the life after death question on your own. But it may be so basic and so simple that it is eluding you. And known multitudinous answers only lead you to greater doubt, more questions, more theories, and more speculation. Believe me; the answer is within each of us. There is no need to ask anyone else, or to expect an answer from anyone to satisfy us. Answers abound. The question is, "Which. if any, do we accept?"

There are so many options, but are they logical? Have too many drawn their own conclusions, while pooh-poohing yours and others that have been offered? If my offering does not interest you, or you find it to be illogical, please look deeper within yourself.

Since you now know where you and I are going, I'd like to add a little levity to this conversation by telling you who I want to be—

"WAITIN' AT THE GATE"

I wonder who will be waitin' at 'The Gate,'
Besides, Saint Peter, who will deliver my fate,
The biggest shock would be, if no one was there,
Would it mean that no one really did care?
That would be like having no mother to
deliver me at birth,
When I first arrived; landed on earth,
If I had my druthers, I know who I would want
to be there,
But would they want to be at the gate;
would they care?
Besides my Mom, I'd put my pets at the front
of the line,
They wouldn't have to think it over; their loyalty
would still be mine,
I would demand instant hugs, licks, and kisses from
my pets; their love of old,
And ask forgiveness, for the many times
I did punish and scold,
Next would be my closest family and friends,
For me, this will be the time their passing away,
ends,

I have no doubt, that there will be laughter,
mingled with tears,
Lost warmth, and love, and joy will
replace their resting years,
If I have my way, there will be a crowd at 'The Gate,'
For reunions can never come too late,
Of course, not everyone can be first; some will have
to wait a little longer,
Perhaps their love was lesser, rather than stronger,
And, obviously, those I do not desire to meet at all
will have the longest wait,
Love will be the key, define the order, and who, I
want to be . . .

"WAITIN' AT THE GATE"

I know now and have known for years, ***"We are the Galaxies."*** We were born of stars and will return upon death to them. And I hope with the following statement, that I have answered all skeptics who deny Jesus' words. ***"In my Father's house are many rooms: if it were not so, I would have told you . . ." (John 14:2 NIV).*** **The rooms exist. They are stars—our Heavenly homes. And yes, there are rooms *for all* in God's endless mansion in space.**

Many years ago, I wrote a poem about my Hereafter home. I loved that poem. It is called—

"TWINKLELAND"

I would like to claim Twinkleland for my own,
However, worldwide astrologers and astronomers
would deny me, their theories yet known,
For I would know the answers they search
for every day,

I would own the stars and join them where
they live and play,
I could enjoy close-up the *Novas* and *Supernovas,* and
learn the secrets of *Black Holes*,
Ride some shooting stars; investigate
my Twinkleland resident's roles,
Oh, the secrets I would find,
Ones that have yet to engage any scientist's mind,
I'm sure my Twinkleland would be filled
with pleasures,
And I would chatter forever about all its treasures,
Its rainbows, fires like hearth flames,
diamonds one and all,
Those that ignite anew, when humans return, after
they answer 'the call,'
If you believe as I, we were each born from a star,
That end is a beginning, when we travel afar,
We live our life on earth,
Then, return to give our star rebirth,
Return its sparkle; rekindle its twinkle, its heartbeat,
Sharing a lovely, silent, melodic treat,
Announcing, 'I have returned to join
Twinkleland's chorus,
A continuous, 'Sanctus, Sanctus, Dominous,'
Joyous, Joyous,
What's that you say? It's a Fairyland,
Maybe so, but it is part of Heaven, and
yes it's grand, my—

"TWINKLELAND"

Now, that I have revealed my theory about where we go after we die, there should be no need to fear death. Come, come . . .

"Walk with me in heavenly sublime. Be a star and light the night. Shine for all to see and let them know that you are there. And that your spirit is waiting for all those who wish to get together in love and friendship. Take time to reminisce, enjoy moments of earthly pleasure, then live together as of old for all Eternity"

I believe we are recycled. We are not waste, but valuable creations. We will live again to be sent where we are needed, probably to perform tasks we know.

We will build on our past lives. We will continue to learn in new Assignments all we can about who we are, what we are, and where we are, until our time once again runs out, and we return to our assigned star in God's mansion in the sky.

How and when will this occur? I cannot answer that because a Heavenly transition will always remain undefined, particularly in relation to earthly time. Why not join me in my cradle fair. It is known as,

"THE HEREAFTER . . ."

Where are you, oh, spirits of the past?
I have just returned; I'm here at last,
Hoping to rekindle the love we once knew,
A love known, individually, only by each one of you,
I've missed you over the years,
As attested too, by my tears,
Please rally round, and I will introduce you to those
you do not know,
Those I met after you left, as I continued to grow,
For that, I will momentarily have to become
a *'Spirit Centipede,'*
Just to accomplish that wonderful deed,

Come, rally round, O, loves, of the past,
And let this very special moment forever last,
For I do not know in everlasting life, if memory
will be as of old,
That I've never been privy too; never been told,
Many say, 'When we die, that's the end,'
Well, I don't believe that, my friend,
For a human is too magnificent a creation to
simply die and fade away forever,
We must live on, and on, and on, and die away
never,
That's what 'Everlasting Life,' means,
Changing form in a new world with new scenes,
We will become spirits of the wild,
Become once again as young as a vibrant child,
Perhaps to retain all the knowledge we gained,
Perhaps only 'the good' will be retained,
Spirits we will be, temporarily,
Giant wheels of spokes creating a new world history,
'The Hereafter' is not an end,
It is a beginning, my friend,
We are not going to be tied to a permanent tether,
I don't expect our "Next Assignment" to last forever,
No, we will move into another "Assignment,"
another "Adventure" to be sure,
For we are resilient, made to live, live
and live, and endure,
Be it known, get ready, spirit life will pick up
pace ~ be faster,
We have much to accomplish, but then again, who
am I to say what will be in . . .

"THE HEREAFTER"

Before I move on and give you my address, I must share something funny with you. At least I found it to be funny. As I was travelling on the staircase, something strange caught my eye. As I turned to look, I realized what it was. I saw a shooting star. It was a very special shooting star. It made me laugh out loud. It was my ***Aunt Net*** travelling to visit my ***Aunt Bella***. How about that? They didn't see me however. If this be commonplace, can you imagine the shooting star traffic on celebrated holidays? I can just hear them yelling, "Step aside, coming through!" O, what joy.

Now, I really wish I knew how far I will have to travel from here, before I will be able to finally step into my star home. But don't worry, if you care to visit, my

Heavenly Celestial Star Crib address is:
4542400453211143473298B

Whenever you have time, join me. I will be waiting for you; always there shining, when I am home. This time upon my return, I might even show myself, as who I am—mischievous me. I am looking forward to misbehaving in a manner not expected of a star. You can count on me for that, if you can find me. Just look up any day, I promise I'll be there. However, I intend to temporarily turn off my twinkle. So it will be a challenge and require a great deal of imagination. For I will turn into,

Jeanette Dowdell

"A STAR IN SILHOUETTE"

"A twinkling star is to motion, what rolling thunder is to noise. It's the chatter and laughter of children while playing with their toys."

Catch a star in silhouette?
You never have, I'll bet,
Is that possible, I wonder?
Perhaps somewhere in its land of thunder,
That place where stars swirl, run and roam free,
While awakening and dying in a mighty
bombastic spree,
Can a renegade non-twinkling star rest on
a bright spot?
Not knowing it's in silhouette, and has become
an attractive pulsating dot,
How wonderful it is to fly among the stars,
To stop off along the way and visit Jupiter and Mars,
I now have met people long gone,
Some, I have even wished upon,
For I believe this to be true,
I was born from a star's very hue,
And now that I have passed on, and left the earth,
My spirit has returned to its original place of birth,
To twinkle once again in heaven's night,
To delight children, as they enter their
dream-zone twilight,
And somewhere in the millennium of my new time,
I'll find some memory sweet,
That quickens my twinkle, as I recall past moments
divine on some human street,
But now, just for you, I will retain my shape and
dim my twinkle; I'll purposefully forget,
So that you will see something extremely rare, me, as,
A star in silhouette

Ah, the Journey—I haven't said much about "The Journey—Life." Nor have I delved specifically into what I meant by "Our Next Assignment, Our Next Grand Adventure." But, I will now. *Eternal Life is the Real Thing.* We are part of God and God is part of us. Each of us is a Cathedral of that spirit which is God—God ever present. That is `why life continues after death—our spirits never die; they become spirits of tomorrow's future and part of a new journey, a new adventure to be lived and enjoyed. Most of us know the abbreviation ***RIP (Rest In Peace)***. It appears on many graves. But my ***RIP*** abbreviation means more. It has a deeper meaning for me. It means ***Restore In Preparation***. Rest, restore, revive and get revved up for Our Next Assignment, which brings with it as many questions as this book holds. And those questions became quite clear to me, before I began this journey home. I questioned death and what it would be like. Even though I don't want to forget life as I know it now. Here are some of the questions I asked myself as I gave deeper thought to my earthly life. I embraced the world around me sighing and relishing each thought and memory. I always recognized and acknowledged not only bits and pieces, but the whole of life—remembering it with pleasure and saying, "Ah, the Journey."

Will death be dark and cold?
Or, filled with warmth and light?
Will it end as quickly as closing my eyes at night?
Will the deep of the unknown suddenly
engulf my being?
Or, will that occur with my last breath?
Will, as some believe, the end will be the end
without
a new tomorrow?
I believe on the other side of the end is a new
beginning,
Just as my *earthly* beginning began from an end,

Death begins another adventure,
And based upon our known life,
what an adventure it will be,
A life filled with challenge—
spectacular dusks and dawns,
Moving round and about,
Meeting new people and learning every day,
Why am I continuing to learn, if I will simply
fade away?
No, my tomorrow will hold new life,
Who knows—another world, another universe,
a new unknown?
Life after death will set its own tone,
Do you believe we'll start again?
If so, will you remain prone?
Or, will you rise and stand tall in your new home?
If we retain the same curiosity as in the life we now
know, what could be better?
But for now, it's life as we know it, without
guarantee,
Tomorrow can hold in its optimism,
total mystique, a new beginning,
After all, profoundly speaking, tomorrow is
tomorrow,
But, today is today,
And in each case, I say . . . *Ah, the journey*

So then, what will our Next Assignment be? Who will decide? Will it be me, or my Maker? Will it be based upon what I have learned in the past? Will it reflect my last known life, or lives? Those we may have lived before, those not necessarily on earth? Perhaps time spent in another world, another universe, another galaxy? Who knows? And, will we remember any past life or lives that we may have lived?

I believe we are not just sent to earth "to be." We are not sent for one purpose, but many purposes. That is why lives are not constant—status quo. They fill voids, help others to fulfill their purpose and reverse negative trends. When people slip between the cracks, we are sent to fill those cracks. A piece of us is part of all who come in contact with us, as we live our lives. Even in a fleeting moment of time we become one. Perhaps just in an instant, a moment of eye contact. Perchance, we met on a prior Assignment.

What do you think? What do you believe?

I believe that we will be sent on many Assignments to fulfill many purposes. And when we complete each Assignment, we return home to rest, regroup and go forth again.

I would like to believe that we will be given an opportunity to have some input into our next Assignment, whatever it might be. However, that may simply be wishful thinking. It may be more cut and dried. We may simply be directed to go and do. And even if we were given a choice of our new Assignment, might it not be tainted by some old thoughts and actions should they somehow remain intact. I wonder.

Years ago, I interviewed a gentleman, whom I asked, "What would you like your life after death to be? He replied, without hesitation, "I want to do whatever I can to help, wherever I am needed. That goes not only for today, but forever."

Now it is my turn to ask that question of myself. For, I am dead. And, I have just arrived at the "Pearly Gates" in the mists of the unknown. My spirit is intact, but it is filled with great innocence and frailty. In this land of veiled mystery I now stand immobile. I am waiting with great expectations for the awakening of my deep faith, as known in the life I just lived.

Who am I to say what Our Next Assignment, Our Next Grand Adventure will I be? I cannot list individually any "Assignments," but I know they all will be as wonderful as the ones lived before.

After all, we must remember who we are. We are stars returning home to occupy our assigned space in the Heavens, returning home to our place of rejuvenation. I am sure that we will be given time to reconnect and enjoy those we wish to engage again from days gone by, before we must leave on another Assignment. How wonderful, and what a comfort to know our Everlasting life includes shoreless sequels.

I hope that you have found this interpretation to be interesting, and worthy of your most valuable possession, your time. And too, I hope that you find some comfort in my thoughts and deeper beliefs for your tomorrow.

It seems an eternity since I stepped upon this staircase to Heaven, but it has been quite a journey. I knew immediately when my transition from *earthly* to *Heavenly* existence became reality, when I felt the staircase upon which I have been travelling noticeably slowing down. And the hand-steps of those who helped me in life were growing fewer in number.

Now suddenly, I am standing on the threshold of my new Eternal Life. I have reached my destination with my present Assignment and Adventure complete. I can feel the breeze of the "Pearly Gates" swinging open, and I know exactly what I have to do. What I have to say, as I walk through.

Nothing profound, just something warm and simple . . .

"Hi, I'm home!"

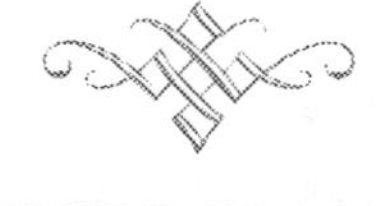

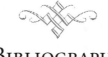

Bibliography

My full-life experience

Biblical References

New International Version of the Holy Bible, (John 14:1-4, Luke 23:42-43 NIV). Scripture taken from the HOLY BIBLE, NEW INTERNATIONAL VERSION, Copywrite © 1973, 1978, 1984, International Bible Society. Used by permission of Zondervan Bible Publishers."

New Revised Standard Version of the Bible (John 14:2 NRSV) and ***Revised Standard Version*** (John 14:2 RSV, revised 1952 A.D.). Scripture quotations are from New Revised Standard Version of the Bible, copyright © 1989 National Council of the Churches of Christ in the United States of America. Used by permission.

New American Bible, St. Joseph Edition (John 14:2 NAB). Scripture text in this work is taken from the *New American Bible,* revised edition © 2010, 1991, 1986, 1970 Confraternity of Christian Doctrine, Washington, D.C. and are used by permission of the copyright owner.

New King James Version (NKJV)—Copyright © 1982 by Thomas Nelson, Inc., Division of Harper Collins Publishers/(KJV) New York, Harper & Brothers, Publishers. Used by permission. All rights reserved.

Scientific American Magazine, 2004

____, Dick, Steven J., "The Transit of Venus"
____, Gerber, J. "How Do Scientists Know the Composition of Earth's Interior?"
____, Llyod, Seth and Ng, Jack, "Black Hole Computers"
____, Minkel JR, "Mars—Foreshadowing Flashes in the Planum"
____, News Scan, "Big Beyond Pluto" California Institute of Technology
____, News Scan, Astronomers may have found the first objects in the universe that generate their own light. European Southern Observatory announcement,
____, "Saturn Unveiled"
____, Stover, Dawn, Popular Science Editor, "The Ring Leader"
____, Venezeano, Gabriele, "the myth of The Beginning of TIME" 2004

nineplanets.org—9/15/12

____, Earth—"Terra, Sol III"
____, Jupiter—"The Bringer of Jollity"
____, Mars—"The Bringer of War"
____, Mercury—"The Winged Messenger"
____, Neptune—"The Mystic"
____, Pluto—"Mathews: Pluto—The Renewer"
____, Saturn—"The Bringer of Old Age"
____, Sun—"Sol"
____, Uranus—"The Magician"
____, Venus—"The Bringer of Peace"

World Book Online 2004—"Meteor"—http://www.aolsvc.Worldbook.aol.com

***CICLOPS* (Cassini Imaging—Central Laboratory for OPerationS) 2000, 2002, 2003, 2004**

Porco, Carolyn, Team Leader—"Cassini Imaging" (Saturn, Jupiter, Titan—Saturn's Largest Moon)—http://ciclops.lpl.arizona.edu

____, "The Greatest Jupiter Portrait"
____, "Portal View—Saturn"
____, "The Veils of Titan"

***http://news*.national geographic.com 2004**

Venus' Moon Pairing Tonight: "Special Treat" for sky watchers

Discover Magazine, 2004

____, "Burdick, Alan, "Seeding the Universe"
____, Gutrel, Fred, "Mission to Mercury"—Discover Magazine
____, "Mackensie, Dana, "Here Comes the Sun"
____, "Saturn Spectacular"
____, Squyres, Steve, "Mars Rover Guru Astonished"
____, "Svitil, Kathy A., "Beyond Pluto" and "Darkness Demystified"
____, "Venus Blots the Sun"
____, "Weinstock, Maia, "Cassini Watch: Saturn's Rings in Technicolor"
____, Wright, Karen, "Black Holes Made Here"

Britt, Robert Roy, Sr. Science Writer, ***http://space.come* science astronomy/hubble**—Sedna 2004

____, "Jupiter's Spots Disappear Amid Major Climate Change"
____, "Weird Object Beyone Pluto Gets Stanger"

http://space.come scienceastronomy/Jupiter—spots

____, "101 Amazing Earth Facts" 2003
____, "Happy 14th Birthday Hubble" 2/22/04
____, "How the Scum of the Earth Led to Advanced Life"
____, "New Case of Oldest Life on Earth"

David, Leonard, Sr., Space Writer, "Venus Revisited: Modern Technology Sharpens Images from Soviet Missions"

____, "Life Zone on Venus Possible" 2003

Natural History 2003, 2004-5,

____, Goldsmith, Donald, "Bolts from Beyond" 2003
____, Liu, Charles, "Let's Make a Galaxy" 2003
____, "Secrets of Shooting Stars" 2003
____, Tyson, Neil de Grasse, "Ringside Seat" and "Vagabonds of Space" 2004
____, Zarnecki, John C., "Destination: Titan"

Time Magazine—2004, 2005, 2012

____, Chang, Kenneth, "Vogager I Approaching Edge of the Solar System"
____, Cray, Dan/Pasadena, and Scherer, Michael and Rogers, Alex/Washington,"
____, Kluger, Jeffrey, "Secrets of the Rings"—What Cassini Discovered When It Got to Saturn and the Wonders It May Uncover In the Mission to Come"
____, Lemonick, Michael D., "Next Stop Pluto"—2005
____, Mallon, Jeffrey and Lubet, "Use Pluto's dwarf status to think big"

Author's Biography

After a lifetime of deep faith, searching for answers, and teaching, Jeanette has come to know, innate or learned, "We are our belief." As we mature, soul-stirring thoughts of tomorrow become paramount. Those thoughts, led to dedicated, prolific writing in many genres. Native Brooklynite, now residing on Long Island, NY